BBC goodfood eatwell

FASTING DAY RECIPES

D0774237

000000744237

10 9 8 7 6 5 4 3 2 1

BBC Books, an imprint of Ebury Publishing
20 Vauxhall Bridge Road,
London SW1V 2SA

BBC Books is part of the Penguin Random House
global.penguinrandomhouse.com

Penguin
Random House
UK

Photographs © BBC Worldwide, 2015
Recipes © BBC Worldwide, 2015
Book design © BBC Worldwide, 2015

First published by BBC Books in 2015

www.eburypublishing.co.uk

A CIP catalogue record for this book is available from the British Library

ISBN 9781849908986

Printed and bound by Firmengruppe APPL, aprinta druck, Wemding, Germany
Colour origination by Dot Gradations Ltd, UK

Commissioning editor: Lizzy Gray
Editorial manager: Lizzy Gaisford
Project editor: Helena Caldon
Designers: Interstate Creative Partners Ltd
Design manager: Kathryn Gammon
Production: Alex Goddard

Penguin Random House is committed to a sustainable future
for our business, our readers and our planet. This book is made
from Forest Stewardship Council® certified paper.

PICTURE AND RECIPE CREDITS

BBC *Good Food* magazine and BBC Books would like to thank the following people for providing photos. While every effort has been made to trace and acknowledge all photographers, we should like to apologize should there be any errors or omissions.

Iain Bagwell p105; Steve Baxter p95; BBC Worldwide p77; Peter Cassidy p133, p159; Dean Grennan p91, p169; Will Heap p29, p145, p157; Amanda Heywood p131; Adrian Lawrence p139; William Lingwood p61; Gareth Morgans p25, p33, p35, p55, p65, p107, p113, p127, p129, p143, p153, p167, p173, p187; David Munns p15, p19, p47, p49, p53, p59, p71, p79, p87, p89, p97, p101, p111, p117, p121, p123, p147, p181; Myles New p31, p41, p43, p51, p99, p109, p125, p163, p179; Stuart Ovenden p21, p57, p189; Lis Parsons p17, p23, p73, p85, p119, p137; Charlie Richards p37, p175; Craig Robertson p81; Howard Shooter p103, p135, p177; Maja Smend p27; Brett Stevens p171; Roger Stowell p75, p141; Sam Stowell p69, p149, p151, p155; Yuki Sugiura p183; Simon Walton p93, p115; Philip Webb p39, p45, p161; Jon Whitaker p185; Frank Wieder p83; Isobel Wield p67.

All the recipes in this book were created by the editorial team at *Good Food* and by regular contributors to BBC magazines.

BBC good food eatwell

FASTING DAY RECIPES

Editor **Kerry Torrens**

BBC BOOKS

Contents

. . . .

Introduction

If you've struggled with your weight for years but love your food, the fasting-day diet might just be the answer. Our selection of recipes has been hand-picked to ensure your fasting meals provide plenty of taste, texture and, above all, satisfaction. So whether you're an experienced cook and love being in the kitchen or can't face the thought of cooking on a fasting day, this little book has the recipes to suit you and your lifestyle.

The fasting-day diet has taken the weight-loss world by storm – and with good reason. Fasting, in some shape or form, has been a popular practice for many hundreds of years and within various cultures. Evidence has been mounting on the health benefits of food restriction – including as an effective means of managing your weight, reducing your risk of diseases, such as diabetes, heart disease and cancer, and potentially strengthening the immune system.

Why our fasting-day recipe book is different

We've designed this book so your fasting days fit easily into your lifestyle – eat when it suits you by selecting recipes according to what you fancy and the calorie count. If you're trying to balance this way of eating with feeding a family, then we've got plenty of recipes that are sure to become family favourites, including our Veggie breakfast bakes and Cheesy bean & sweetcorn cakes with salsa. Throughout the book you'll find tips for adapting recipes to suit the non-fasting members of your family – that way you won't need to spend hours in the kitchen preparing multiple meals. Similarly, if you have weight-conscious friends we've included a selection of sharing dishes so your social life doesn't have to stop just because you're fasting.

If, like many of us, you're often short of time and need something quick, easy and straight from the cupboard, you'll love our *Omelette in five*, our freeze-ahead soups, including our *Springtime minestrone*, and our speedy salads – especially our unusual, but delicious, *Stir-fried salad with almonds*.

What's it all about?

If you're following the fasting-day diet you eat normally for 5 days and then for 2 days you eat about a quarter of your usual calorie intake – that's roughly 600 calories for men and 500 for women. Many fasters prefer to select two non-consecutive days of the week, when they know their social commitments are likely to be lighter – Monday and Thursday are often popular days.

Our fasting-day recipes include lean protein (meat, poultry, fish, eggs, dairy, beans and pulses) to keep you full and satisfied, as well as some slow-burn carbs (wholegrains) to keep you energized. If you stick to the amounts we've suggested, there's no need for complicated calculations or weighing because we've done all the hard work for you.

The main aim of the fasting-day diet is to achieve an extended food-free period. That's because it's during this break for the digestive system that the health benefits of the diet are achieved. It can be tough, going for extended periods without eating, especially when you're restricting energising carbs. That's why we've included a handful of fasting-day recipes that are under 100 calories – ideal for when you just need that little something. We've also based some of our fasting-day recipes on healthy carbs, like our *Quinoa, lentil & feta salad* and our *Smoky prawns with green couscous*.

Filling foods for fasting days

When you're cutting down on calories, even for a couple of days, it's important to eat a wide variety of foods to ensure you're getting all the nutrients your body needs. Our recipes are packed with plant foods like beans, pulses, fruit and veg, so they're brimming with vitamins, minerals and phyto-nutrients. All these are essential for keeping you in tip-top health as well as helping you get your 5-a-day. We've also ensured there's a good proportion of protein in our recipes, so you'll feel satisfied even though the calorie count is low. Egg-based dishes are especially useful, because eggs have been proven to keep you fuller for longer, which means you're likely to want fewer calories later in the day.

Don't forget that even low-calorie dishes should contain some fat, and that's because certain nutrients, such as vitamins A, D, E and K, are fat-soluble, so they need to be eaten with fat for the body to absorb them. We've included 'good' fats from nuts, seeds, olives and oily fish, and slashed the saturated-fat count (typically found in full-fat dairy and processed red meat). All of our recipes are cooked from scratch, with some taking just a few minutes. The main benefit of this is that you'll be reducing your intake of trans fats (manmade hard fats), found in processed and packaged foods.

We've not forgotten that an important consideration for anyone on the fasting-day diet is taste, so we've ensured all our recipes have full-on flavour. So whether it's flavours from zesty citrus fruits, such as lemon and lime, or tangy herbs and spices, including garlic, ginger and chilli, all of our recipes are designed to give your taste buds a workout!

Remember, these low-calorie dishes are aimed at all of us who want to lose weight or enjoy lighter meals for a couple of days a week. We wouldn't recommend sticking with them day after day on a long-term basis. Anyone on medication, or with diabetes, pregnant women, young adults and children should consult their GP before starting a calorie-restrictive diet.

Kerry

Kerry Torrens
Good Food magazine

Notes &
conversion tables

· ·

NOTES ON THE RECIPES
- Eggs are large in the UK and Australia and extra large in America unless stated.
- Wash fresh produce before preparation.
- Recipes contain nutritional analyses for 'sugar', which means the total sugar content including all natural sugars in the ingredients, unless otherwise stated.

OVEN TEMPERATURES

GAS	°C	°C FAN	°F	OVEN TEMP.
¼	110	90	225	Very cool
½	120	100	250	Very cool
1	140	120	275	Cool or slow
2	150	130	300	Cool or slow
3	160	140	325	Warm
4	180	160	350	Moderate
5	190	170	375	Moderately hot
6	200	180	400	Fairly hot
7	220	200	425	Hot
8	230	210	450	Very hot
9	240	220	475	Very hot

APPROXIMATE WEIGHT CONVERSIONS
- All the recipes in this book list both metric and imperial measurements. Conversions are approximate and have been rounded up or down. Follow one set of measurements only; do not mix the two.
- Cup measurements, which are used in Australia and America, have not been listed here as they vary from ingredient to ingredient. Kitchen scales should be used to measure dry/solid ingredients.

Good Food is concerned about sustainable sourcing and animal welfare. Where possible, humanely reared meats, sustainably caught fish (see fishonline.org for further information from the Marine Conservation Society) and free-range chickens and eggs are used when recipes are originally tested.

SPOON MEASURES

Spoon measurements are level unless otherwise specified.

- 1 teaspoon (tsp) = 5ml
- 1 tablespoon (tbsp) = 15ml
- 1 Australian tablespoon = 20ml (cooks in Australia should measure 3 teaspoons where 1 tablespoon is specified in a recipe)

APPROXIMATE LIQUID CONVERSIONS

METRIC	IMPERIAL	AUS	US
50ml	2fl oz	¼ cup	¼ cup
125ml	4fl oz	½ cup	½ cup
175ml	6fl oz	¾ cup	¾ cup
225ml	8fl oz	1 cup	1 cup
300ml	10fl oz/½ pint	½ pint	1¼ cups
450ml	16fl oz	2 cups	2 cups/1 pint
600ml	20fl oz/1 pint	1 pint	2½ cups
1 litre	35fl oz/1¾ pints	1¾ pints	1 quart

Indian-summer salad

An Indian-style salad that's packed with vitamins and minerals. Keep leftovers for serving as an accompaniment to meat or fish on non-fasting days.

 20 minutes 6

- 3 carrots
- 1 bunch radishes
- 2 courgettes
- ½ small red onion
- small handful mint leaves

FOR THE DRESSING
- 1 tbsp white wine vinegar
- 1 tsp Dijon mustard
- 1 tbsp mayonnaise
- 2 tbsp olive oil

1 Grate the carrots into a large bowl. Thinly slice the radishes and courgettes, and finely chop the onion. Mix all the vegetables together in the bowl with the mint leaves.

2 Whisk together the vinegar, mustard and mayonnaise for the dressing until smooth, then gradually whisk in the oil. Add salt and freshly ground black pepper to taste, then drizzle over the salad and mix well before serving.

PER SERVING 79 kcals, protein 1g, carbs 5g, fat 6g, sat fat 1g, fibre 2g, sugar 6g, salt 0.35g

Courgette & tomato soup

Make this soup in late summer or early autumn when courgettes and tomatoes are plentiful and cheap. It freezes well, so prepare a big batch for a fasting-day fall-back.

 45 minutes   8

- 1 tbsp butter
- 2 onions, chopped
- 1kg/2lb 4oz courgettes, sliced
- 1kg/2lb 4oz tomatoes, chopped
- 2 tbsp plain flour
- ½ tsp turmeric powder
- 2 litres/3½ pints chicken or vegetable stock from cubes

1 Melt the butter in a large pan, add the onions and courgettes, and cook for 5 minutes on a medium heat, stirring occasionally.

2 Add the tomatoes and flour. Cook for a couple of minutes, stirring to stop the flour becoming lumpy. Add the turmeric and stock, then cover and simmer for 30 minutes.

3 Purée the soup in a blender, or with a handheld stick blender, then push it through a sieve, if you want a really smooth texture. Serve, or chill and then freeze for up to 2 months.

PER SERVING 90 kcals, protein 4g, carbs 12g, fat 3g, sat fat 1g, fibre 4g, sugar 8g, salt 0.8g

Hot & sour broth with prawns

This tasty light dish can be knocked up in 15 minutes. If you're cooking for non-fasters, serve yourself then add a handful of cooked noodles and heat through.

 15 minutes   4

- 3 tbsp rice vinegar or white wine vinegar
- 500ml/18fl oz chicken stock
- 1 tbsp reduced-salt light soy sauce
- 1–2 tbsp golden caster sugar
- thumb-sized piece ginger, peeled and thinly sliced
- 2 small hot red chillies, deseeded and thinly sliced
- 3 spring onions, thinly sliced
- 300g/10oz small raw peeled prawns

1 Put the vinegar, stock, soy sauce, sugar (start with 1 tablespoon and add the second at the end, if you want the soup sweeter), ginger, chillies and spring onions in a pan, and bring to a simmer.
2 Cook for 1 minute, then add the prawns to heat through. Serve in small bowls or cups.

PER SERVING 93 kcals, protein 17g, carbs 5g, fat 1g, sat fat none, fibre none, sugar 5g, salt 1.39g

Crab & asparagus salad with chilli & lime dressing

Asparagus is rich in folic acid and a good source of soluble fibre, which helps keep you full. You'll only need half the dressing for this; keep the rest for a salad the next day.

 15 minutes 2

- 100g/4oz asparagus tips
- 1 large handful baby leaf spinach
- ¼ cucumber, cut into ribbons with a peeler
- 50g/2oz white crab meat

FOR THE DRESSING

- juice 1 lime
- 1 tbsp olive oil
- 2 tbsp rice wine vinegar
- pinch sugar
- 1 tsp Thai fish sauce
- 1 red chilli, deseeded and finely chopped

1 Cook the asparagus in plenty of boiling salted water until tender, about 3 minutes, then drain and cool under running water. Set aside on kitchen paper to absorb any excess water.
2 To make the dressing, combine all the ingredients in a small bowl and set aside.
3 Arrange the spinach and cucumber on two plates, then scatter over the asparagus and crab meat. Drizzle over half the quantity of dressing just before serving; reserve the remainder for the next day.

PER SERVING 88 kcals, protein 8g, carbs 3g, fat 5g, sat fat 1g, fibre 2g, sugar 2g, salt 1.1g

Smoked-salmon & avocado sushi

The combination of protein and carbs means a couple of these delicious rolls will keep you full for a while. Make a day ahead for ease and convenience.

 30 minutes 32

- 300g/10oz sushi rice
- 2 tbsp rice vinegar or white wine vinegar
- 1 tsp caster sugar
- 1 large avocado
- juice ½ lemon
- 4 sheets nori seaweed
- 4 large slices smoked salmon
- 1 bunch chives

1 Put the rice in a small pan with 600ml/ 1 pint water. Bring to the boil and cook for 10 minutes until the water is absorbed and the rice is tender. Stir through the vinegar and sugar, then cover and cool.

2 Skin, stone and slice the avocado. Put in a bowl and squeeze over the lemon juice.

3 Divide the rice among the nori sheets and spread it out evenly, leaving a 1cm/½in border at the top and bottom. Lay the salmon over the rice, followed by lengths of chives, and finally position the avocado across the centre.

4 Fold the bottom edge of the seaweed over the filling, then roll it up firmly. Dampen the top border with a little water to help it seal the roll. Repeat to make four rolls. The rolls can now be wrapped individually in cling film and chilled until ready to serve.

5 Using a serrated knife, cut each roll into eight rounds and enjoy.

PER SUSHI 49 kcals, protein 2g, carbs 7g, fat 2g, sat fat none, fibre 1g, sugar none, salt 0.24g

Warm chicken-liver salad

· ·

This really is a superfood salad – a good source of iron, folic acid and vitamin C that's also low in fat. Tuck in!

 25 minutes    2

- 75g/2½oz fine green beans
- 100g/4oz chicken livers, trimmed
- 1 tsp olive oil
- pinch chopped fresh or dried rosemary leaves
- ½ whole chicory or Baby Gem lettuce, separated into leaves
- 50g/2oz watercress
- 1 tbsp balsamic vinegar

1 Cook the green beans in a pan of boiling water for 3 minutes, drain and keep warm. Meanwhile, toss together the chicken livers, olive oil and rosemary. Heat a large non-stick pan and cook the chicken livers over a high heat for 5–6 minutes until nicely browned and cooked through – they should still be a little pink in the centre.

2 Arrange the beans on serving plates with the chicory or lettuce leaves and watercress. Add the vinegar to the pan, cook for a couple of seconds then spoon over the salad and top with the chicken livers.

· ·
PER SERVING 92 kcals, protein 10g, carbs 4g, fat 3g, sat fat 1g, fibre 2g, sugar 3g, salt 0.1g

Veggie breakfast bakes

Who says being on a diet means giving up a cooked breakfast? For the rest of the family make this meaty but healthy with a low-fat sausage or some turkey bacon.

 45 minutes 4

- 4 large field mushrooms
- 8 tomatoes, halved
- 1 garlic clove, thinly sliced
- 2 tsp olive oil
- 200g bag leaf spinach
- 4 eggs

1 Heat oven to 200C/180C fan/gas 6. Put the mushrooms and tomatoes into four ovenproof dishes. Divide the garlic among the dishes, drizzle over the oil and some seasoning, then bake for 10 minutes.
2 Meanwhile, put the spinach into a large colander, then pour over a kettle of boiling water to wilt it. Squeeze out any excess water, then add the spinach to the dishes.
3 Make a little gap between the vegetables and crack an egg into each dish. Return to the oven and cook for a further 8–10 minutes or until the egg is cooked to your liking.

PER SERVING 127 kcals, protein 9g, carbs 5g, fat 8g, sat fat 2g, fibre 3g, sugar 5g, salt 0.4g

Spiced parsnip & cauliflower soup

This soup freezes beautifully, so make a double batch if your pans are big enough!

 1 hour 5 minutes 6

- 1 tbsp olive oil
- 1 medium cauliflower, cut into florets
- 3 parsnips, peeled and chopped
- 2 onions, peeled and chopped
- 1 tbsp fennel seeds
- 1 tsp coriander seeds
- ½ tsp turmeric powder
- 3 garlic cloves, sliced
- 1–2 green chillies, deseeded and chopped
- 5cm/2in piece ginger, peeled and sliced
- zest and juice 1 lemon, plus more juice to taste
- 1 litre/1¾ pints vegetable stock
- handful coriander leaves, chopped

1 Heat the oil in a large pan and add the vegetables. Partially cover the pan and sweat the veg for 10–15 minutes until soft but not brown.

2 In a separate pan, dry-roast the spices with a pinch of salt for a few minutes until fragrant. Grind with a pestle and mortar to a fine powder.

3 Add the garlic, chilli, ginger and ground spices to the vegetables, and cook for about 5 minutes, stirring regularly. Add the lemon zest and juice. Pour in the stock, topping up if necessary just to cover the veg. Simmer for 25–30 minutes until all the vegetables are tender.

4 Purée with a blender until smooth. Dilute the consistency with more water if needed, until you get a thick but easily pourable soup. Season generously, stir in the coriander and add more lemon juice to balance the taste. Serve straight away or chill in the fridge and reheat. Finish with an extra grind of black pepper, if you like. Freeze any extra soup in individual portions for future fast days.

PER SERVING 133 kcals, protein 7g, carbs 18g, fat 4g, sat fat 1g, fibre 9g, sugar 11g, salt 0.6g

Thai pumpkin soup

Make the most of the autumn abundance of squash and pumpkins. The Thai curry paste adds a kick here, making this a satisfying, warm and welcoming lunch.

 1 hour 5 minutes   6

- 1.5kg/3lb 5oz pumpkin or squash, peeled, deseeded and roughly chopped
- 4 tsp sunflower oil
- 1 onion, sliced
- 1 tbsp grated ginger
- 1 lemongrass stalk, bashed a little
- 3–4 tbsp Thai red curry paste
- 400ml can reduced-fat coconut milk
- 850ml/1½ pints vegetable stock
- 1 red chilli, deseeded and sliced, to garnish (optional)

1 Heat oven to 200C/180C fan/gas 6. Toss the pumpkin or squash in a roasting tin with half the oil and some seasoning, then roast for 30 minutes until the chunks are golden and tender.

2 Meanwhile, put the remaining oil in a pan with the onion, ginger and lemongrass. Gently cook for 8–10 minutes until softened. Stir in the curry paste for 1 minute, followed by the roasted pumpkin or squash, all but 3 tablespoons of the coconut milk and the stock. Bring to a simmer, cook for 5 minutes, then scoop out the lemongrass. Cool for a few minutes, then whizz the soup until smooth with a hand-held blender, or in a large blender in batches.

3 Return to the pan, as necessary, to heat through and season, to taste. Serve drizzled with the remaining coconut milk and scattered with chilli, if you like.

PER SERVING 146 kcals, protein 4g, carbs 10g, fat 9g, sat fat 5g, fibre 4g, sugar 7g, salt 0.7g

Quick gazpacho

This is a delicious, healthy chilled soup that's perfect for hot summer days.

 10 minutes   1

- 1 red pepper
- 1 red chilli
- 225ml/8fl oz passata
- 1 garlic clove, crushed
- 1 tsp sherry vinegar
- juice ½ lime

1 Peel the skin off the red pepper with a vegetable peeler, remove the seeds and chop up the flesh. Cut the chilli in half, scrape away the seeds and chop the flesh.

2 In a blender (or with a stick blender), whizz together the passata, chopped red pepper, chopped chilli, the garlic, sherry vinegar and lime juice until smooth. Season to taste and chill until cold. Serve in a soup bowl with a few ice cubes.

PER SERVING 126 kcals, protein 5g, carbs 26g, fat 1g, sat fat none, fibre 3g, sugar 18g, salt 1.26g

Springtime minestrone

This simple soup will become a fasting-day favourite in no time – it makes a great standby for a quick and easy lunch. Freeze any leftovers in individual portions.

 10 minutes   4

- 200g/8oz mixed green vegetables (we used asparagus, broad beans and spring onions)
- 700ml/1¼ pints hot vegetable stock
- 140g/5oz cooked pasta (spaghetti chopped into small pieces works well)
- 215g can butter beans, drained and rinsed
- 3 tbsp green pesto

1 Put the green vegetables in a medium-sized pan, then pour over the stock. Bring to the boil, then reduce the heat and simmer until the vegetables are cooked through, about 3 minutes.
2 Stir in the cooked pasta, the beans and 1 tablespoon of the pesto. Warm through, then ladle into bowls and top each with a drizzle of the remaining pesto.

PER SERVING 125 kcals, protein 8g, carbs 16g, fat 4g, sat fat 1g, fibre 4g, sugar 3g, salt 0.7g

Mediterranean sardine salad

This super-quick, no-cook supper is heart-healthy and a good source of omega-3 and calcium. Leftovers can be packed up for a satisfying take-to-work lunch next day.

 15 minutes 2

- ½ x 90g bag salad leaves
- small handful pitted black olives, roughly chopped
- ½ tbsp capers, drained
- 120g can sardines in tomato sauce, drained and sauce reserved
- 2 tsp olive oil
- 2 tsp red wine vinegar

1 Divide the salad leaves between two plates, then sprinkle over the olives and capers.
2 Roughly break up the sardines and add to the salad. Mix the tomato sauce with the oil and vinegar, and drizzle the dressing over the salad.

PER SERVING 142 kcals, protein 12g, carbs 1g, fat 10g, sat fat 2g, fibre 1g, sugar 1g, salt 0.7g

Chicken noodle soup

This fragrant soup is perfect when you crave something satisfying yet light. It's great when cooking for others, too – just top up the bowls of non-fasters with extra noodles.

 30 minutes 4

- 1.3 litres/2¼ pints chicken stock
- 2 star anise
- 2.5cm/1in piece ginger, peeled and sliced
- 2 garlic cloves in skins, bruised
- 2 pak choi, shredded
- 85g/3oz medium egg noodles
- 4 spring onions, finely sliced
- 100g/4oz cooked chicken, torn into very thin shreds
- splash reduced-salt light soy sauce
- handful basil leaves
- 1 mild plump red chilli, deseeded and finely sliced

1 Pour the stock into a medium pan. Add the star anise, ginger and garlic, and gently simmer, without boiling, for 10 minutes. For the last 2 minutes, put the pak choi into a colander or sieve, suspend it over the pan and cover to steam the greens.

2 Drop the egg noodles into the stock, stirring to separate, then simmer for 4 minutes until tender. Throw in the spring onions and chicken. Season to taste with a splash of soy sauce. Ladle the soup into bowls and scatter over the pak choi, basil leaves and chilli.

PER SERVING 132 kcals, protein 19g, carbs 5g, fat 4g, sat fat 1g, fibre 1g, sugar 3g, salt 1.08g

Asian chicken salad

Spicing up a low-calorie meal with some fresh hot chilli is a great way to make it more satisfying.

 20 minutes 🥧 2

- 1 boneless skinless chicken breast
- 1 tbsp Thai fish sauce
- zest and juice ½ lime (about 1 tbsp)
- 1 tsp caster sugar
- 100g bag mixed salad leaves
- large handful coriander leaves, roughly chopped
- ¼ red onion, thinly sliced
- ½ red chilli, deseeded and thinly sliced
- ¼ cucumber, sliced

1 Put the chicken in a pan and cover with cold water, bring to the boil, then cook for 10 minutes. Remove from the pan and tear into shreds.

2 To make the dressing, stir together the fish sauce, lime zest, juice and sugar in a small bowl until the sugar dissolves.

3 Put the mixed leaves and coriander in a salad bowl, then top with the chicken, onion, chilli and cucumber. Pour the dressing over the salad and toss through just before serving.

PER SERVING 109 kcals, protein 19g, carbs 6g, fat 1g, sat fat none, fibre 1g, sugar 5g, salt 1.6g

Summer eggs

Brunch, lunch or dinner – take your pick with this easy, flexible one-pan meal. What's more, eggs are packed with benefits that protect skin from UV ageing.

 18 minutes 2

- 1 tbsp olive oil
- 400g/14oz courgettes (about 2 large), chopped into small chunks
- 200g pack cherry tomatoes, halved
- 1 garlic clove, crushed
- 2 eggs
- few basil leaves, to garnish

1 Heat the oil in a non-stick frying pan, then add the courgettes. Fry for 5 minutes, stirring every so often until they start to soften.

2 Add the tomatoes and garlic, then cook for a few minutes more. Stir in a little seasoning, then make two gaps in the mix and crack in the eggs.

3 Cover the pan with a lid or a sheet of foil, then cook for 2–3 minutes until the eggs are done to your liking. Scatter over a few basil leaves and serve.

PER SERVING 196 kcals, protein 12g, carbs 7g, fat 13g, sat fat 3g, fibre 3g, sugar 6g, salt 0.25g

Moroccan-spiced cauliflower & almond soup

This soup is deliciously creamy with a spicy kick. Make a batch and freeze it.

 30 minutes 4

- 1 large cauliflower
- 2 tbsp olive oil
- ½ tsp each ground cinnamon, cumin and coriander
- 2 tbsp harissa paste, including garnish
- 1 litre/1¾ pints hot vegetable stock
- 50g/2oz toasted flaked almonds, including garnish

1 Cut the cauliflower into small florets.
2 Heat the oil in a large pan, add the spices and most of the harissa paste, and fry for 2 minutes. Add the cauliflower florets, hot vegetable stock and most of the almonds. Cover and cook for 20 minutes until the cauliflower is tender.
3 Blend the soup until smooth, then serve in warmed bowls with the rest of the harissa and a sprinkle of the remaining toasted almonds on top.

PER SERVING 200 kcals, protein 8g, carbs 10g, fat 14g, sat fat 2g, fibre 5g, sugar 7g, salt 1g

Green cucumber & mint gazpacho

This cool, refreshing soup makes a welcome light lunch on a hot summer's day and provides four of your 5-a-day. If you like a spicy kick, add more Tabasco to taste.

 20 minutes, plus chilling   2

- 1 cucumber, halved lengthways, deseeded and roughly chopped
- 1 yellow pepper, deseeded and roughly chopped
- 2 garlic cloves, crushed
- 1 small ripe avocado, chopped
- bunch spring onions, chopped
- small bunch mint leaves, chopped
- 150g pot fat-free natural yogurt
- 2 tbsp white wine vinegar
- few shakes green Tabasco sauce
- snipped chives, to garnish

1 In a food processor or blender, blitz all the ingredients except the chives, reserving half the mint and yogurt, until smooth. Add a little extra vinegar, Tabasco and some seasoning to taste, then a splash of water, if you like a slightly thinner soup.

2 Chill until very cold, then serve with a dollop more of the remaining yogurt, a sprinkling of the reserved mint and the chives, plus a few ice cubes, if you like. The soup will keep in the fridge for 2 days – just give it a stir before you serve.

PER SERVING 186 kcals, protein 8g, carbs 15g, fat 11g, sat fat 2g, fibre 5g, sugar 14g, salt 0.28g

Spicy harissa, aubergine & chickpea soup

If you're not so keen on spicy food, add a dollop of fat-free Greek yogurt to the soup bowls as you serve. This soup freezes well so reserve any leftovers for future fast days.

 50 minutes   4

- 1 onion, chopped
- 1 tbsp olive oil
- 2 tbsp harissa paste
- 2 aubergines, diced
- 400g can chopped tomatoes
- 400g can chickpeas, drained and rinsed
- 2 tbsp chopped coriander leaves

1 Soften the onion in the oil in a large pan. Add the harissa and cook for 2 minutes, stirring. Add the aubergine and coat in the harissa.

2 Add the chopped tomatoes, chickpeas and 500ml/18fl oz water. Bring to the boil and simmer for 30 minutes.

3 Stir through the chopped coriander, season and serve.

PER SERVING 157 kcals, protein 6g, carbs 20g, fat 5g, sat fat 1g, fibre 9g, sugar 8g, salt 0.7g

Crab & noodle soup

This dish is so quick and easy it'll become a fasting-day favourite in no time!

 8 minutes   2

- 50g/2oz thin rice noodles
- 100g/4oz Chinese-style stir-fry mixed vegetables
- 2 tsp Thai fish sauce
- 2 tsp sweet chilli sauce
- 600ml/1 pint vegetable stock
- 170g can white crabmeat in brine, drained
- handful coriander leaves, roughly chopped, to garnish

1 Put the noodles and vegetables into a bowl, then pour over boiling water to cover. Leave to soak for 4 minutes, covered in cling film, until the noodles are tender and the vegetables are just softened.

2 Heat together the fish sauce, chilli sauce and stock in a pan. Drain the noodles and veg from their soaking water and divide between two serving bowls. Add the crabmeat and pour over the hot stock. Scatter with chopped coriander to serve.

PER SERVING 184 kcals, protein 17g, carbs 28g, fat 1g, sat fat none, fibre 3g, sugar 5g, salt 2.66g

Crab & sweetcorn chowder

· ·

This quick soup is delicious all year round, but in summertime swap the canned corn for fresh niblets, sliced straight off the cob.

 35 minutes   4

- 1 onion, finely chopped
- 1 leek, green and white parts separated and sliced
- 2 carrots, chopped
- 850ml–1 litre/1½ pints–1¾ pints low-sodium chicken or vegetable stock
- 1 medium potato, peeled and diced
- 198g can sweetcorn kernels, drained
- 170g can white crabmeat in brine, drained
- 3 tbsp half-fat crème fraîche
- 1 tsp snipped chives

1 Put the onion, the white part of the leek and the carrots in a large pan, and pour on a few tablespoons of the stock. Cook over a medium heat for about 10 minutes, stirring regularly until soft. Add a splash more stock if the vegetables start to stick.

2 Add the potato, green leek parts and most of the remaining stock, and simmer for 10–15 minutes, until the potato is tender.

3 Tip in the drained sweetcorn and crabmeat, then cook for a further 1–2 minutes. Remove from the heat and stir in the crème fraîche and some seasoning. Add the rest of the stock if the soup is too thick. Sprinkle with the chives and serve. Freeze leftovers in single portions for a handy fasting-day fall-back.

· ·
PER SERVING 200 kcals, protein 10g, carbs 26g, fat 5g, sat fat 2g, fibre 6g, sugar 12g, salt 1.2g

Chickpea, tomato & spinach curry

This well-balanced, superhealthy curry is suitable for vegans and contains two of your 5-a-day. You can substitute any canned beans for the chickpeas.

 55 minutes 6

- 1 onion, chopped
- 2 garlic cloves, chopped
- 3cm/1¼in piece ginger, peeled and chopped
- 6 ripe tomatoes, chopped
- ½ tbsp oil
- 1 tsp ground cumin
- 2 tsp ground coriander
- 1 tsp turmeric powder
- pinch chilli flakes
- 1 tsp yeast extract (we used Marmite)
- 4 tbsp red split lentils
- 6 tbsp coconut cream
- 1 broccoli head, broken into small florets
- 400g can chickpeas, drained and rinsed
- 100g bag baby leaf spinach
- 1 lemon, halved
- 1 tbsp each toasted sesame seeds and chopped cashew nuts

1 Put the onion, garlic, ginger and tomatoes in a food processor or blender, and whizz to a purée.

2 Heat the oil in a large pan. Add the spices, fry for a few seconds and add the purée mixture and yeast extract. Bubble together for 2 minutes, then add the lentils and coconut cream. Cook until the lentils are tender, then add the broccoli and cook for 4 minutes. Stir in the chickpeas and spinach, squeeze over the lemon halves and swirl through the sesame-and-cashew mixture, to serve.

PER SERVING 199 kcals, protein 8g, carbs 18g, fat 10g, sat fat 5g, fibre 5g, sugar 6g, salt 0.42g

Charred aubergine, pepper & bulghar salad

A great summer lunch or, if calories allow, serve alongside a grilled skinless chicken breast, small salmon fillet or lean fillet steak for a more substantial dinner.

 20 minutes 4

- 175g/6oz bulghar wheat
- 2 tbsp sundried tomato paste
- 4 baby aubergines, each sliced lengthways into 3
- 1 red pepper, deseeded and cut into 1cm-/½in-thick slices
- 2 tsp olive oil
- handful basil leaves

1 Prepare the bulghar according to the pack instructions. Tip into a large bowl and stir through the tomato paste. Season well.
2 Heat a barbecue or griddle pan. Drizzle the aubergines and red pepper with the oil and cook for 5 minutes on each side until lightly charred.
3 Stir the aubergines and red pepper into the bulghar mixture, then season and stir through the basil to serve. Save any leftovers for lunch next day.

PER SERVING 198 kcals, protein 6g, carbs 38g, fat 3g, sat fat none, fibre 6g, sugar 6g, salt 0.2g

Open prawn-cocktail sandwich

Open sandwiches are great for dieters. Take a thin slice of wholegrain bread, load with salad and a tasty topping and you have a substantial yet low-calorie lunch.

 15 minutes   2

- 2 tbsp extra-light mayonnaise
- 1 tbsp reduced-sugar tomato ketchup
- 2 tbsp chopped dill leaves
- 1 lemon, cut into 8 wedges
- 100g pack cooked peeled prawns
- ½ cucumber, deseeded and diced
- 2 handfuls cherry tomatoes, halved
- 2 thin slices wholemeal or rye bread
- 25g bag rocket leaves

1 Make a dressing in a medium bowl by mixing together the mayonnaise, ketchup, half the dill, the juice from 4 of the lemon wedges and some seasoning. Toss in the prawns, cucumber and tomatoes.

2 Arrange the bread on two plates, top each with rocket and pile on the prawn filling. Scatter with the remaining dill and serve with the remaining lemon wedges, for squeezing over.

PER SERVING 173 kcals, protein 17g, carbs 22g, fat 3g, sat fat none, fibre 3g, sugar 7g, salt 1.6g

Salmon, strawberry & fennel salad

This stylish salad with its unusual combination of smoked salmon and strawberries is sure to tantalize the taste buds.

 15 minutes 2

- 75g/2½oz smoked salmon, torn into strips
- 1 small fennel bulb, trimmed, cored, halved and finely sliced into strips
- 25g/1oz rocket leaves
- 100g/4oz ripe strawberries, hulled and halved

FOR THE DRESSING
- 2 tbsp olive oil
- 1 tbsp white wine vinegar
- 1 tsp wholegrain mustard
- ½ tsp clear honey

1 In a small bowl, whisk together the dressing ingredients, season and set aside.
2 Put the smoked salmon, fennel, rocket and strawberries into a separate bowl.
3 Drizzle the dressing over the salad and toss gently so everything glistens. Finish with a grinding of black pepper and serve.

PER SERVING 200 kcals, protein 11g, carbs 7g, fat 13g, sat fat 2g, fibre 4g, sugar 6g, salt 2g

Chinese steamed bass with greens

. . . .

Steaming is one of the healthiest ways to cook (see p92) – this recipe packs in the flavour with less than 200 calories per serving. It's also a good source of omega-3.

 20 minutes   2

- 2 sustainable bass or other white fish fillets, about 100g/4oz each
- 1 red or green chilli, deseeded and finely chopped
- 1 tsp peeled and finely chopped ginger
- 300g/10oz green cabbage or other greens, finely shredded
- 2 tsp rapeseed oil
- 1 tsp sesame oil
- 2 garlic cloves, thinly sliced
- 2 tsp reduced-salt light soy sauce

1 Sprinkle the fish with the chilli, ginger and a little seasoning. Steam the cabbage or greens for 5 minutes. Lay the fish on top of the cabbage and steam for a further 5 minutes or until cooked through.

2 Meanwhile, heat the oils in a small pan, add the garlic and quickly cook, stirring until lightly browned. Transfer the cabbage and fish to serving plates, sprinkle each with 1 teaspoon of the soy sauce, then pour over the garlicky oil.

. . . .

PER SERVING 188 kcals, protein 23g, carbs 8g, fat 8g, sat fat 1g, fibre 4g, sugar 7g, salt 0.74g

Ham & beetroot salad bowl

Vary this salad by replacing the ham with any of the following: cooked turkey breast, flaked poached salmon, cooked peeled prawns or a little crumbled goat's cheese.

 15 minutes   2

- 100g/4oz frozen peas
- 175g/6oz cooked beetroot, diced
- 2 spring onions, thinly sliced
- 2 tbsp low-fat Greek yogurt
- 2 tsp horseradish sauce
- ½ iceberg lettuce, shredded
- 100g/4oz wafer-thin sliced ham, torn into strips

1 Pour boiling water over the peas and leave for 2 minutes, then drain well.
2 Tip the peas, beetroot and spring onions into a bowl, and mix well. In a small bowl, mix the yogurt and horseradish, then add about 1 tablespoon boiling water to make a dressing.
3 Pile the lettuce into two bowls, then spoon over the beetroot mix. Thinly drizzle the dressing over the salad and top with the ham, to serve.

Mediterranean vegetables with lamb

This is a great summer stew, just add a green salad and serve it to non-fasting members of the family with couscous, rice or even jacket potatoes.

🕐 45 minutes   4

- 1 tbsp olive oil
- 250g/9oz lean lamb fillet, trimmed of any fat and thinly sliced
- 140g/5oz shallots, halved
- 2 large courgettes, cut into chunks
- ½ tsp each ground cumin, paprika and ground coriander
- 1 red, 1 orange and 1 green pepper, deseeded and cut into chunks
- 1 garlic clove, sliced
- 150ml/¼ pint vegetable stock
- 250g/9oz cherry tomatoes
- handful coriander leaves, roughly chopped

1 Heat the oil in a large heavy-based frying pan. Cook the lamb and shallots over a high heat for 2–3 minutes until golden. Add the courgettes and stir-fry for 3–4 minutes until beginning to soften.

2 Add the spices and toss well, then add the peppers and garlic. Reduce the heat and cook over a moderate heat for 4–5 minutes until the peppers start to soften.

3 Pour in the stock and stir everything to coat. Add the tomatoes, season, then cover with a lid and simmer for 15 minutes, stirring occasionally, until the veg are tender. Stir through the coriander. This stew freezes well, so any leftovers can be frozen in individual portions for future fasting days.

PER SERVING 192 kcals, protein 17g, carbs 11g, fat 9g, sat fat 3g, fibre 4g, sugar 10g, salt 0.25g

Spicy Moroccan eggs

Eggs keep you fuller longer, which is ideal when you are dieting; they're a good source of choline, which boosts memory, and the yolk is packed with bone-building vitamin D.

 30 minutes 4

- 2 tsp rapeseed oil
- 1 large onion, halved and thinly sliced
- 3 garlic cloves, sliced
- 1 tbsp rose harissa paste
- 1 tsp ground coriander
- 150ml/¼ pint vegetable stock
- 400g can chickpeas
- 2 x 400g cans cherry tomatoes
- 2 courgettes, finely diced
- 200g bag baby leaf spinach
- 4 tbsp chopped coriander leaves
- 4 eggs

1 Heat the oil in a large deep frying pan and fry the onion and garlic for about 8 minutes, stirring every now and then until starting to turn golden. Add the harissa and ground coriander, stir well then pour in the stock and chickpeas with their liquid. Cover and simmer for 5 minutes, then mash about a third of the chickpeas to thicken the stock a little.

2 Tip the tomatoes and courgettes into the pan and cook gently for 10 minutes until the courgettes are tender. Fold in the spinach so that it wilts into the mix.

3 Stir in the coriander then make four hollows in the mixture and break in the eggs. Cover and cook for 2 minutes then take off the heat and allow to settle for another 2 minutes before serving.

PER SERVING 242 kcals, protein 16g, carbs 22g, fat 10g, sat fat 2g, fibre 8g, sugar 11g, salt 1g

Preserved-lemon & tomato salad with feta

Light and crunchy, tart and fruity, this simple Moroccan salad is deliciously refreshing served on its own on fast days or enjoyed as part of a vegetarian spread the next day.

 15 minutes 4

- 4 large tomatoes, deseeded and cut into thick strips
- 1 large red onion, thinly sliced
- 1 preserved lemon, pulp removed and rind cut into thin strips, or grated zest 1 lemon
- 200g pack feta
- 2 tbsp olive oil
- juice ½ lemon
- small bunch each flat-leaf parsley and mint, leaves finely shredded

1 Put the tomatoes, onion and lemon rind or zest in a shallow bowl or on a platter. Crumble the feta over, drizzle with oil and lemon juice, and scatter over the parsley and mint.

2 Toss gently just before serving. The salad keeps well, covered and chilled in the fridge.

PER SERVING 215 kcals, protein 10g, carbs 9g, fat 16g, sat fat 7g, fibre 2g, sugar 7g, salt 1.49g

Lemony potato, broccoli & goat's-cheese salad

This salad is perfect for making ahead, but take it out of the fridge a good hour before serving to allow the flavours to develop.

 35 minutes, plus cooling 2

- 140g bag new potatoes
- 2 tsp extra-virgin olive oil
- zest and juice ½ lemon
- ½ broccoli head, cut into florets
- 100g/4oz green beans, trimmed
- handful dill, leaves roughly chopped
- 50g/2oz goat's cheese
- 1 tbsp toasted pine nuts

1 Boil the potatoes for 12–15 minutes until tender. Mix together the oil, lemon zest and juice in a serving bowl. Lift out the potatoes with a slotted spoon, leaving the pan of water on the hob. Drain the potatoes well, then put them in the serving bowl and stir to mix with the lemon and oil. Leave on one side to cool.

2 Add the broccoli and beans to the pan of boiling water. Cook for 4 minutes until tender but still with some bite. Drain, then cool under cold running water.

3 Stir the drained broccoli and beans into the cooled potatoes with the dill and some seasoning. Break the goat's cheese into chunks and scatter over the vegetables with the pine nuts and serve.

PER SERVING 248 kcals, protein 12g, carbs 15g, fat 14g, sat fat 5g, fibre 7g, sugar 3g, salt 0.5g

Crunchy detox salad

The vibrant colours, textures and flavours of this fabulous salad make it ideal for a lunch box. It keeps in the fridge for up to 3 days – just give it a stir before serving.

 20 minutes 4

- 250g/9oz broccoli, cut into small florets
- 100g/4oz ready-to-eat dried apricots, cut into strips
- 300g/10oz red cabbage, finely shredded
- 400g can chickpeas, drained and rinsed
- 50g/2oz sunflower seeds
- 1 small red onion, finely sliced
- 2cm/¾in piece ginger, grated
- juice 1 small orange
- 1 tbsp balsamic vinegar
- 2 tsp olive oil

1 Blanch the broccoli in a pan of boiling water for 1 minute. Drain and quickly cool under cold running water, then pat dry with kitchen paper. Put in a salad bowl with the apricots, red cabbage, chickpeas and sunflower seeds.

2 Put the onion and ginger in a small bowl with the orange juice, vinegar and oil. Mix well. Leave for 5 minutes to soften the onion, then add to the salad and thoroughly toss everything together to serve.

PER SERVING 248 kcals, protein 12g, carbs 28g, fat 11g, sat fat 1g, fibre 9g, sugar 16g, salt 0.38g

Stir-fried salad with almonds

A stir-fried salad may sound strange, but take the pan off the heat before you add the leafy salad ingredients and you'll love the fresh-tasting result.

 15 minutes   2

- 2 tbsp olive oil
- 25g/1oz whole blanched almonds
- ½ bunch spring onions, sliced
- ½ small cucumber, deseeded and sliced
- 2 celery sticks, cut into batons
- 175g/6oz small tomatoes, quartered
- 1 Little Gem lettuce, torn in pieces
- 25g/1oz watercress
- ½ small bunch coriander
- 1 tsp lemon juice
- pinch sugar

1 Heat 1 tablespoon of the oil in a frying pan or wok and fry the almonds for 2–3 minutes until golden. Drain on kitchen paper then chop roughly.

2 Add the remaining oil to the pan or wok and, when hot, add the spring onions, cucumber, celery and tomatoes, and stir-fry for 2 minutes. Remove from the heat, add the remaining ingredients and toss together until combined. Season.

3 Spoon the warm salad on to serving plates and scatter over the almonds. Spoon over the pan juices and serve.

PER SERVING 237 kcals, protein 6g, carbs 8g, fat 19g, sat fat 2g, fibre 4g, sugar 7g, salt 0.1g

Ratatouille

A tasty summery lunch or supper that's high in fibre and vitamin C, and provides four of your 5-a-day. Make up a big batch and freeze ahead.

 45 minutes 4

- 2 red or yellow peppers
- 4 large ripe tomatoes
- 5 tbsp olive oil
- 2 large aubergines, cut into large chunks
- 4 small courgettes, thickly sliced
- 1 medium onion, thinly sliced
- 3 garlic cloves, crushed
- 1 tbsp red wine vinegar
- 1 tsp sugar
- small bunch basil, leaves torn

1 Peel the peppers using a potato peeler then remove the seeds and cut into large chunks. Set aside.

2 Score a small cross on the base of each tomato, then cover with boiling water. Leave for 20 seconds, then cool in a bowl of cold water. Peel, deseed and roughly chop the flesh. Set aside.

3 Heat 2 tablespoons of oil in a large frying pan then brown the aubergines for 5 minutes all over, until soft. Remove to a plate then fry the courgettes in another tablespoon of the oil for 5 minutes or until golden. Add the peppers and onion, then the garlic and fry for a further minute.

4 Stir in the vinegar and sugar, then tip in the tomatoes and half the basil. Return the rest of the vegetables to the pan with some salt and black pepper, and cook for 5 minutes. Serve with the remaining basil scattered over.

PER SERVING 241 kcals, protein 6g, carbs 20g, fat 16g, sat fat 2g, fibre 8g, sugar 18g, salt 0.05g

Herby mushroom pasta

Low in calories and rich in energizing B vitamins, mushrooms give a lovely rich flavour to this simple pasta dish.

 20 minutes 2

- 250g/9oz field or portobello mushrooms, thickly sliced
- 2 tsp wholegrain mustard
- 3 garlic cloves, sliced or crushed
- 150ml/¼ pint vegetable stock (from a cube is fine)
- 200g/8oz penne (or other tube pasta shapes)
- 3 tbsp flat-leaf parsley, chopped
- zest 1 lemon

1 Put the mushrooms, mustard, garlic and vegetable stock into a frying pan, bring to the boil and simmer for 5 minutes or until the stock has nearly all evaporated and the mushrooms are soft.

2 Meanwhile, cook the pasta according to the pack instructions. Drain and toss with the mushrooms, parsley and lemon zest. Season to taste and serve straight away.

PER SERVING 235 kcals, protein 9g, carbs 49g, fat 2g, sat fat 0.2g, fibre 3g, sugar 2g, salt 0.25g

Crustless vegetable quiche

· ·

As the name suggests there's no pastry, just chunky vegetables set in egg. Save any leftovers for the next day's lunch.

 40 minutes 4

- 1 tbsp vegetable oil
- 1 yellow and 1 orange pepper, cut into quarters and deseeded
- 2 courgettes, cut into chunks
- 2 large red onions, cut into wedges
- 4 medium eggs, beaten
- 100ml/3½fl oz milk
- 2 tbsp fresh vegetarian pesto sauce
- crisp green leaf salad, to serve (optional)

1 Heat oven to 200C/180 fan/gas 6. Heat the oil in a wok or large frying pan and stir-fry the peppers, courgettes and onions over a high heat for 2–3 minutes.

2 Transfer the vegetables to an oiled 2-litre ovenproof dish. In a large bowl, mix together the eggs, milk, pesto and some seasoning.

3 Pour the egg mix over the vegetables and bake for 25 minutes until firm to the touch in the centre. Serve warm with a crisp green leaf salad, if you like.

· ·

PER SERVING 211 kcals, protein 9g, carbs 10g, fat 15g, sat fat 3g, fibre 2g, sugar 10g, salt 0.36g

Smoked trout & cucumber open sandwiches

· ·

Trout is fabulous – it is an excellent source of those all-important omega-3 oils yet lower in calories than salmon.

 20 minutes 2

- 125g pack skinless hot-smoked trout fillets
- ½ x 250g tub Quark
- ½–1 tsp horseradish sauce
- squeeze lemon juice
- 2 small slices granary bread
- ¼ cucumber, sliced
- 25g/1oz watercress
- 2 handfuls cherry tomatoes

1 Flake the fish into a large bowl, then stir in the Quark and the horseradish sauce to taste. Season the pâté with some black pepper and the squeeze of lemon juice.
2 Toast the bread, then top each piece with cucumber slices and watercress. Spoon half the trout pâté on top of each and serve with the cherry tomatoes on the side.

· ·

PER SERVING 225 kcals, protein 26g, carbs 19g, fat 5g, sat 1g, fibre 3g, sugar 5g, salt 1.7g

Prawn, pea & tomato curry

A spicy dish that's packed with flavour and contributes to your 5 a day. For non-fasters serve with rice - if you're fasting you'll find the peas make a great substitute!

 20 minutes   2

- 2 tsp olive or rapeseed oil
- 1 onion, halved, cut into 6 wedges
- 3 ripe tomatoes, each cut into 8 wedges
- small piece ginger, peeled and chopped
- 3 garlic cloves, roughly chopped
- 1–2 tbsp curry paste (we used tikka masala paste)
- 200g/8oz raw peeled king prawns
- 100g/4oz frozen peas
- ½ small bunch coriander, leaves chopped, to garnish

1 Heat the oil in a frying pan, then fry the onions over a medium heat until soft and beginning to brown, for about 5 minutes. Meanwhile, reserve a couple of the tomato wedges then whizz the remainder in a food processor with the ginger and garlic.

2 Add the curry paste to the pan for about 30 seconds. Stir through the tomato mix and remaining tomato wedges, then bubble over a high heat for 5 minutes, stirring so the sauce doesn't catch. Mix in the prawns and peas; simmer until the prawns are pink and cooked through. Scatter with coriander and serve.

PER SERVING 227 kcals, protein 23g, carbs 16g, fat 6g, sat fat 1g, fibre 6g, sugar 10g, salt 0.8g

Asian prawn & pineapple salad

Just toss this together and enjoy – instead of prawns you could flake leftover roast chicken or smoked mackerel through this sweet-tasting salad.

 20 minutes 4

- 1 small pineapple or 350g/12oz pineapple chunks
- 140g/5oz beansprouts
- 250g/9oz cooked, peeled king prawns
- ½ cucumber, peeled, deseeded and sliced on the angle
- 200g/8oz cherry tomatoes, halved
- handful mint leaves, roughly chopped
- 50g/2oz unsalted cashew nuts, toasted

FOR THE DRESSING

- ½ red chilli, deseeded and sliced
- 1 garlic clove
- 1 tsp golden caster sugar
- juice 2 limes
- 1½ tsp Thai fish sauce

1 Mash the chilli, garlic and sugar for the dressing to a paste using a pestle and mortar or small food processor. Stir in the lime juice.

2 Peel, quarter, core and slice the pineapple at an angle. Toss with the beansprouts, prawns, cucumber, tomatoes and some of the dressing. Pile into bowls and scatter with the mint and cashews. Drizzle with the rest of the dressing and serve. Any leftovers can be covered and kept in the fridge for the next day.

PER SERVING 202 kcals, protein 19g, carbs 17g, fat 7g, sat fat 1g, fibre 3g, sugar 14g, salt 1.5g

Smoky prawns with green couscous

The citrusy dressing adds a fresh, clean-tasting flavour to this quick couscous salad.

 25 minutes ⏏ 2

- 100g/4oz large raw peeled prawns
- zest and juice 1 lemon, plus extra wedges to garnish
- 1 garlic clove, crushed
- 1 tsp paprika
- 1 tbsp olive oil
- 85g/3oz couscous
- 2 courgettes, sliced on the diagonal
- small bunch coriander, leaves only, chopped

1 Tip the prawns into a small bowl. Add all the lemon zest, plus most of the lemon juice, the garlic, paprika and half of the oil. Mix, then set aside. Make the couscous according to pack instructions, cover and leave for 10 minutes.

2 Heat a non-stick frying pan, then add 1 tablespoon of the prawn marinade, the courgettes and a splash of water. Stir-fry for 4–5 minutes until the courgettes are golden, then tip on to a plate. Add the prawns to the pan with the remaining marinade, then fry for 1 minute until just pink.

3 Fluff up the couscous with a fork, then mix in the courgettes, coriander, remaining oil and lemon juice and some seasoning. Scrape in the prawns with all the pan juices and toss briefly before serving with extra lemon wedges for squeezing.

PER SERVING 225 kcals, protein 15g, carbs 24g, fat 7g, sat fat 1g, fibre 2g, sugar 3g, salt 0.26g

Steamed bass with pak choi

. . . .

This one-pot dish is cooked in a Chinese bamboo steamer. If you don't have a steamer, cook it in a foil parcel in a medium oven for 30 minutes.

 15 minutes   2

- small piece ginger, peeled and sliced
- 2 garlic cloves, finely sliced
- 3 spring onions, finely sliced
- 2 tbsp reduced-salt light soy sauce
- 1 tbsp sesame oil
- 2 sea bass fillets, about 140g/5oz each
- 2 pak choi heads, quartered

1 In a small bowl, combine all of the ingredients, except the fish and the pak choi, to make a soy mix. Line one tier of a two-tiered bamboo steamer loosely with foil. Lay the fish, skin-side up, on the foil and spoon over the soy mix. Put the fish over a pan of simmering water and throw the pak choi into the second tier then cover it with a lid. Alternatively, add the pak choi to the fish layer after 2 minutes of cooking – the closer the tier is to the steam, the hotter it is.

2 Leave everything to steam for 6–8 minutes until the pak choi has wilted and the fish is cooked. Divide the greens between two plates, then carefully lift out the fish. Lift up the foil and drizzle the tasty juices back over the fish.

. . . .

PER SERVING 230 kcals, protein 30g, carbs 5g, fat 9g, sat fat 1g, fibre 2g, sugar 3g, salt 2.1g

Baked fish with Thai spices

Snapper or sea bass work equally well in this recipe, although trout is a more cost-effective option and complements the aromatic flavours of the Thai spices.

 20 minutes 4

- 4 trout fillets, about 200g/8oz each
- 1 lemongrass stalk, finely chopped
- small piece ginger, peeled and finely chopped
- 1 red chilli, deseeded and finely chopped
- 1 garlic clove, finely chopped
- 1 tbsp Thai fish sauce
- juice 2 limes
- 1 tsp golden caster sugar
- handful coriander, leaves roughly chopped

1 Heat oven to 200C/180C fan/gas 6. Tear off two large sheets of foil and put one fillet, skin-side down, in the centre of each sheet. Make a sauce by mixing together the remaining ingredients. Spoon half of the sauce over the fillets.

2 Put the other two fish fillets on top of each fillet to make a sandwich, skin-side up, then tightly seal the foil to create two packages. Bake in the oven for 12–15 minutes. Bring the packages to the table to open and serve with the rest of the sauce. For non-fasters serve with steamed rice.

PER SERVING 236 kcals, protein 40g, carbs 2g, fat 8g, sat fat 2g, fibre none, sugar 1g, salt 1.02g

Skinny pepper, tomato & ham omelette

Eggs are packed with energizing B vitamins as well as minerals like magnesium, zinc and iron. Using fewer yolks helps to lower the fat content of this tempting omelette.

 25 minutes   2

- 2 whole eggs and 3 egg whites
- 1 tsp olive oil
- 1 red pepper, deseeded and finely chopped
- 2 spring onions, white and green parts kept separate and finely chopped
- 2–3 slices wafer-thin extra-lean ham, shredded
- 25g/1oz reduced-fat mature Cheddar, grated

1 Mix the eggs and egg whites with some seasoning. Heat the oil in a medium non-stick frying pan and cook the pepper for 3–4 minutes. Throw in the white parts of the spring onions and cook for 1 minute more. Pour in the eggs and cook over a medium heat until almost completely set.

2 Sprinkle on the ham and cheese, and continue cooking the omelette until just set in the centre, or flash it under a hot grill, if you like it well done. Serve straight from the pan with the green part of the spring onion sprinkled on top.

PER SERVING 206 kcals, protein 21g, carbs 5g, fat 12g, sat fat 3g, fibre 1g, sugar 5g, salt 1.21g

Turkey & ham salad

Take what's in the fruit bowl and some leftover ham or turkey and you've got a great salad in 15 minutes flat. If you're taking it to work, add the dressing just before eating.

 15 minutes 2

- 100g bag Continental salad
- 1 ripe pear or crisp apple
- handful chopped walnuts (or use hazelnuts or flaked almonds)
- 2 thin slices each turkey and ham

FOR THE DRESSING
- ½ small red onion, finely chopped
- 2 tsp wine vinegar, any type
- 1 tsp clear honey
- 2 tbsp low-fat natural yogurt

1 Tip the bag of salad on to individual plates. Quarter, core and slice the pear or apple, then scatter the fruit over the salad leaves along with the walnuts.
2 Cut the turkey and ham into strips and scatter over the salad.
3 Mix together all the dressing ingredients in a small bowl, then drizzle over the salad just before serving.

PER SERVING 221 kcals, protein 13g, carbs 17g, fat 10g, sat fat 2g, fibre 4g, sugar 16g, salt 0.9g

Low-fat chicken balti

This recipe is proof that you don't have to give up curries on fasting days!

 1 hour, plus marinating 4

- 450g/1lb boneless skinless chicken breasts, cut into bite-sized pieces
- 1 tbsp lime juice
- 1 tsp each paprika, cumin seeds, turmeric powder, ground cumin, ground coriander and garam masala
- ¼ tsp hot chilli powder
- 1½ tbsp rapeseed oil
- 1 cinnamon stick
- 3 cardamom pods, split
- 1 small–medium green chilli
- 1 onion, coarsely grated
- 2 garlic cloves, very finely chopped
- 2.5cm/1in piece ginger, grated
- 250ml/9fl oz organic passata
- 1 red pepper, deseeded and cut into small chunks
- 1 medium tomato, chopped
- 85g/3oz baby leaf spinach
- handful coriander leaves, to garnish

1 Mix the chicken with the lime juice, paprika, chilli powder and a grinding of black pepper. Marinate for 15 minutes.

2 Heat 1 tablespoon of the oil in a large non-stick pan. Add the cinnamon stick, cardamom pods, whole chilli and the cumin seeds, and stir-fry briefly. Stir in the onion, garlic and ginger, and fry until the onion starts to brown. Add the remaining oil and the chicken and fry until the chicken changes colour. Stir in the turmeric, ground cumin, ground coriander and garam masala for 2 minutes.

3 Pour in the passata and 150ml/¼ pint water, then drop in the chunks of pepper. When starting to bubble, lower the heat and simmer for 15–20 minutes or until the chicken is tender and cooked through.

4 Stir in the tomato, simmer for 3 minutes, then add the spinach and season. If you want to thin down the sauce, splash in a little more water. Scatter with the coriander leaves and serve. Any leftovers can be frozen.

PER SERVING 217 kcals, protein 30g, carbs 10g, fat 7g, sat fat 1g, fibre 3g, sugar 8g, salt 0.5g

Chicken, ginger & green-bean hotpot

A light chicken casserole that makes a great Asian-inspired one-pot – for non-fasters serve the hotpot with steamed rice.

 30 minutes 2

- ½ tbsp vegetable oil
- 2cm/¾in piece ginger, peeled and cut into matchsticks
- 1 garlic clove, chopped
- ½ onion, thinly sliced
- 1 tbsp Thai fish sauce
- ½ tbsp light soft brown sugar
- 250g/9oz skinless chicken thigh fillets, trimmed of all fat and cut in ½
- 125ml/4fl oz chicken stock
- 50g/2oz green beans, trimmed and cut into 2.5cm/1in lengths
- 1 tbsp chopped coriander leaves

1 Heat the oil in a pan over a medium–high heat. Add the ginger, garlic and onion, and stir-fry for about 5 minutes or until lightly golden. Add the fish sauce, sugar, chicken and stock. Cover and cook over a medium heat for 15 minutes.

2 For the final 3 minutes of cooking, add the green beans. Remove from the heat and stir through the coriander.

PER SERVING 215 kcals, protein 30g, carbs 9g, fat 7g, sat fat 1g, fibre 2g, sugar 7g, salt 2g

Oriental chicken & papaya salad

Sesame oil has a wonderful pungent flavour, so you don't need much to make a lively dressing for this fruity chicken salad.

 30 minutes   2

- 3 tsp sesame oil
- 1 tbsp lime juice
- 2 tsp reduced-salt light soy sauce
- 250g/9oz boneless skinless chicken breasts, sliced in strips
- 100g bag rocket, watercress and spinach salad
- ½ bunch spring onions, finely sliced
- ¼ cucumber, deseeded and chopped
- 1 small papaya, peeled, deseeded and sliced

1 Whisk 1 teaspoon of the sesame oil in a small bowl with the lime juice and soy sauce to make a dressing. Set aside.
2 Heat the remaining oil in a frying pan or wok. Tip in the chicken strips and stir-fry for about 8 minutes until golden and cooked, but still moist. Remove from the heat and let the chicken cool for 2–3 minutes.
3 Tip the salad into a large bowl and scatter over the spring onions, cucumber and papaya. Add the chicken and dressing, and toss everything together gently until all the ingredients are well mixed. Serve while the chicken is still warm.

PER SERVING 231 kcals, protein 32g, carbs 10g, fat 6g, sat fat 1g, fibre 3g, sugar 9g, salt 0.8g

Chicken with orange & avocado salsa

· ·

Packing your fasting day with protein keeps you full and satisfied. Lean chicken is protein-packed, while avocados have the highest protein content of any fruit.

 20 minutes 2

- 1 tsp olive oil
- 2 boneless skinless chicken breasts, cut in half on the diagonal
- zest and juice ½ lime
- ½ avocado
- 1 orange
- 1 red chilli, deseeded and diced (optional)
- 2 spring onions, finely sliced
- 1 tsp chopped coriander or torn basil leaves

1 Heat the oil in a non-stick frying pan, season the chicken and fry for 10 minutes, turning once. Add the lime juice for the final minute of cooking.

2 Meanwhile, peel away the skin of the avocado and, with a small knife, cut the flesh into small chunks. Tip into a bowl. Cut away the skin and pith of the orange, cut out the segments, then add to the avocado with the remaining ingredients, not forgetting the lime zest. Toss gently, then serve alongside the chicken.

· ·
PER SERVING 233 kcals, protein 32g, carbs 8g, fat 8g, sat fat 2g, fibre 3g, sugar 7g, salt 0.23g

Lamb kebabs with fennel & cucumber slaw

The crunchy cucumber and fennel salad mixed with low-fat Greek yogurt makes a perfect accompaniment to these juicy grilled kebabs.

 20 minutes  4

- 400g can green lentils, drained and rinsed
- 250g/9oz pack lean minced lamb
- 1 tsp ground coriander
- 1 cucumber, chopped
- 1 fennel bulb, shredded
- 200g pot reduced-fat Greek yogurt
- 1 small garlic clove, crushed (optional)
- 1 mild red chilli, deseeded and chopped

1 Heat grill to high. Put the lentils into the bowl of a food processor, then whizz to a rough paste. Tip hte lentil paste into another bowl, and add the mince, coriander and plenty of seasoning, and mix well. Roll into 16 balls, divide them among four skewers, then grill for 10 minutes, turning halfway through, until golden and juicy in the middle.

2 Meanwhile, mix the cucumber and fennel with the yogurt, garlic (if using), chilli and some salt and black pepper to taste. Serve the slaw with the kebabs. Any extra kebabs can be frozen.

PER SERVING 202 kcals, protein 21g, carbs 12g, fat 8g, sat fat 4g, fibre 3g, sugar 4g, salt 1.02g

Teriyaki steak with fennel slaw

If there are only two of you, halve the number of steaks and marinade, but make the full quantity of slaw and keep it for lunch the following day.

 20 minutes, plus marinating 4

- 2 tbsp reduced-salt dark soy sauce
- 1 tbsp red wine vinegar
- 1 tsp clear honey
- 4 sirloin or rump steaks, trimmed of all visible fat, each about 125g/4½oz

FOR THE FENNEL SLAW
- 1 large carrot, coarsely grated
- 1 fennel bulb, halved and thinly sliced
- 1 red onion, halved and thinly sliced
- handful coriander leaves
- juice 1 lime

1 Mix the soy, vinegar and honey in a dish, then add the steaks and leave to marinate for 10–15 minutes.
2 Toss together the carrot, fennel, onion and coriander for the slaw, then chill until ready to serve.
3 Remove the steaks from the marinade, reserving the marinade. Transfer the steaks to a hot griddle pan and cook for a few minutes on each side, depending on the thickness and how well done you like them. Set the meat aside to rest on a plate, then add the reserved marinade to the pan. Bubble the marinade until it reduces a little to make a sticky sauce.
4 Dress the slaw with the lime juice, then pile on to plates and serve with the steaks. Spoon the sauce over the meat.

PER SERVING 217 kcals, protein 28g, carbs 8g, fat 8g, sat fat 3g, fibre 3g, sugar 7g, salt 1.1g

Beef strips with crunchy Thai salad

Rump steak is a good choice for this dish as it's not too expensive and has plenty of flavour. Trim off any excess fat after grilling.

 10 minutes 2

- 1 thick-cut lean beef steak, about 300g/10oz
- 2 tbsp lime juice
- 2 tsp Thai fish sauce
- 2 tsp light muscovado sugar
- 1 small red chilli, deseeded and finely chopped
- 100g bag crunchy salad mix
- 25g/1oz carrot, grated
- handful beansprouts

1 Heat grill to high. Lightly season the steak, then grill on each side for 2–3 minutes for medium–rare, or longer if you prefer your meat well done.
2 Mix the lime juice, fish sauce, sugar and chilli together in a jug to make a dressing.
3 Tip the salad, carrot and beansprouts into a bowl, then add the dressing, tossing everything together. Divide between two plates.
4 Thinly slice the beef and add to the salad then serve.

PER SERVING 249 kcals, protein 33g, carbs 7g, fat 9g, sat fat 4g, fibre 1g, sugar 6g, salt 1.2g

Italian-style beef stew

Bold flavours make this dish the perfect comfort food for a winter's night. It's low in saturated fat and salt and a good source of vitamin C.

 30 minutes 2

- 140g/5oz beef steak, thinly sliced
- 1 tbsp olive oil
- 1 small onion, sliced
- 1 garlic clove, sliced
- 1 small yellow pepper, deseeded and thinly sliced
- 227g can chopped tomatoes
- 1 rosemary sprig, leaves chopped
- small handful pitted black olives

1 In a large pan, fry the beef slices in oil for 2 minutes until browned. Tip the beef out on to a plate, then add the onion and garlic to the pan, and fry for 5 minutes until softened. Add the pepper, tomatoes and rosemary to the pan, then bring to the boil. Simmer for 15 minutes until reduced.

2 Stir through the beef and the olives, cook for a further 2 minutes then serve.

PER SERVING 242 kcals, protein 16g, carbs 11g, fat 14g, sat fat 4g, fibre 4g, sugar 9g, salt 0.7g

Omelette in five

. . . .

All you need is five ingredients and five minutes, making this the perfect dish for those with little time. You can multiply the ingredients to feed the whole family.

 5 minutes 1

- 2 eggs
- 1 tsp butter
- 1 tbsp grated cheese
- 2 cherry tomatoes, halved
- 1 spring onion, sliced
- green salad, to serve

1 Break the eggs into a bowl and whisk gently with a fork until the white and the yolk are combined.

2 Heat a small frying pan over a medium heat, then add the butter. When the butter has melted and is starting to sizzle, pour in the beaten eggs. Using a spatula, pull the cooked eggs from around the outside of the pan into the middle to allow the runny eggs to cook evenly. Once the eggs are almost set, sprinkle over the cheese, tomatoes and spring onion.

3 Fold one half of the omelette over the other, using a spatula (tilting the pan often helps, too). Lift the omelette on to a plate and serve straight away with a green salad.

. . . .
PER SERVING 266 kcals, protein 18g, carbs 1g, fat 21g, sat fat 8g, fibre none, sugar 1g, salt 0.7g

Cheesy bean & sweetcorn cakes with salsa

. . . .

A vibrant Tex-Mex with a difference – it's good for you! Use strong Cheddar, as a little adds a lot of flavour. Serve to non-fasters in tortillas with salsa and guacamole.

 30 minutes 4

- 400g can mixed beans in water, drained and rinsed
- 400g can chickpeas, drained and rinsed
- 50g/2oz mature Cheddar, grated
- 198g can sweetcorn, drained and rinsed
- 8 jalapeño slices from a jar, finely chopped
- 1 egg, beaten
- small handful coriander leaves, chopped
- 2 tbsp vegetable oil
- 10 cherry tomatoes, quartered
- ½ red onion, sliced
- juice ½ lime
- salad leaves, to serve (optional)

1 Put the beans and chickpeas in the bowl of a food processor and blend until smooth. Tip into another bowl and add the cheese, sweetcorn, jalapeños, egg and half the coriander. Season, mix well to combine, then shape into eight patties.

2 Heat the oil in a large frying pan and cook the patties for 4 minutes on each side – you may have to do this in batches. Keep them warm in the oven as you go.

3 Mix the tomatoes, onion, remaining coriander and the lime juice with a little salt to make a salsa. Serve the cakes with the salsa and some salad leaves, if you like. Keep any remaining cakes for lunch the next day.

. . . .

PER SERVING 292 kcals, protein 17g, carbs 24g, fat 13g, sat fat 4g, fibre 12g, sugar 2g, salt 1.9g

Lentil & red-pepper salad with a soft egg

Just five ingredients and on the table in just fifteen minutes – what could be better?

 15 minutes 2

- 2 eggs
- 400g can green lentils, drained and rinsed
- 1 small red onion, thinly sliced
- 1 red pepper, deseeded and finely chopped
- 1 tbsp balsamic vinegar
- handful rocket leaves
- 1 tbsp olive oil

1 Boil the eggs for 6 minutes, then quickly cool under cold running water and peel off the shells. Tip the lentils into a bowl with the onion, red pepper and balsamic vinegar. Mix well.

2 Put the lentil-and-pepper salad on a serving plate, then pile the rocket on top. Drizzle with the oil, then halve the eggs and sit them on top of the salad to serve.

PER SERVING 284 kcals, protein 17g, carbs 25g, fat 13g, sat fat 3g, fibre 9g, sugar 8g, salt 1.49g

Quinoa, lentil & feta salad

. . . .

Quinoa is a seed, not a grain, so it's packed with protein, making it a filling and satisfying alternative to rice or couscous.

 30 minutes 4

- 200g/8oz quinoa, rinsed
- 1 tsp olive oil
- 1 shallot or ½ onion, finely chopped
- 2 tbsp roughly chopped tarragon leaves
- 400g can Puy or green lentils, drained and rinsed
- ¼ cucumber, peeled and diced
- 100g/4oz feta, crumbled
- 6 spring onions, thinly sliced
- zest and juice 1 orange
- 1 tbsp red or white wine vinegar

1 Cook the quinoa in a large pan of boiling water for 20 minutes until tender, drain well, then set aside to cool.
2 Meanwhile, heat the oil in a small pan, then cook the shallot or onion for a few minutes until softened. Add the tarragon, stir well, then remove from the heat.
3 Stir the softened shallot and tarragon into the cooled quinoa along with the lentils, cucumber, feta, spring onions, orange zest and juice and vinegar. Toss well together and chill until ready to serve. This salad keeps well in the fridge so save any leftovers for the next day's lunch.

. . . .
PER SERVING 286 kcals, protein 16g, carbs 39g, fat 9g, sat fat 3g, fibre 2g, sugar 6g, salt 1.48g

Gnocchi & tomato bake

Making a welcome change from pasta, this dish is deceptively light yet enough for a family supper.

 30 minutes 4

- 1 tbsp olive oil
- 1 onion, chopped
- 1 red pepper, deseeded and finely chopped
- 1 garlic clove, crushed
- 400g can chopped tomatoes
- 500g/1lb 2oz pack gnocchi
- handful basil leaves, torn
- ½ x 125g ball mozzarella, torn into chunks

1 Heat grill to high. Heat the oil in a large frying pan, then soften the onion and pepper for 5 minutes. Stir in the garlic, fry for 1 minute, then tip in the tomatoes and gnocchi, and bring to a simmer. Bubble for 10–15 minutes, stirring occasionally, until the gnocchi is soft and the sauce has thickened. Season, stir through the basil, then transfer to a large ovenproof dish.

2 Scatter with the mozzarella and grill for 5–6 minutes until the cheese is bubbling and golden.

PER SERVING 285 kcals, protein 10g, carbs 50g, fat 7g, sat fat 3g, fibre 4g, sugar 8g, salt 1.64g

Satay noodles with crunchy veg

A satisfying meal with plenty of crunch!

 15 minutes 2

- 1 tbsp crunchy peanut butter
- 1 tbsp sweet chilli sauce
- 1 tbsp reduced-salt light soy sauce
- 150g pack straight-to-wok noodles
- 2 tsp oil
- thumb-sized knob ginger, grated
- ½ x 300g pack stir-fry vegetables
- handful basil leaves
- 25g/1oz roasted peanuts, roughly chopped

1 Mix the peanut butter, chilli and soy sauces in a small bowl with 100ml/3½fl oz hot water to make a smooth satay sauce. Set aside.

2 Put the noodles in a bowl and pour boiling water over them. Stir gently to separate, then drain thoroughly.

3 Heat the oil in a wok, then stir-fry the ginger and harder pieces of veg from the stir-fry mix, such as peppers, for 2 minutes. Add the noodles and the rest of the veg, then stir-fry over a high heat for 1–2 minutes until the veg are just cooked.

4 Push the veg to one side of the pan, then pour the satay sauce into the other side, tilting the pan. Bring to the boil. Mix the sauce with the stir fry, then sprinkle over the basil leaves and peanuts to serve.

PER SERVING 300 kcals, protein 9g, carbs 26g, fat 17g, sat fat 3g, fibre 4g, sugar 9g, salt 1.5g

Vegetable tagine with chickpeas & raisins

· ·

Enjoy a superhealthy meal that's high in fibre, low in fat, saturated fat and salt, while contributing an impressive four of your 5-a-day.

 30 minutes   2

- 1 tbsp olive oil
- 1 onion, chopped
- pinch each ground cinnamon, coriander and cumin
- 1 courgette, cut into chunks
- 1 tomato, chopped
- 210g can chickpeas, drained and rinsed
- 2 tbsps raisins
- 200ml/7floz vegetable stock
- 140g/5oz frozen peas
- chopped coriander leaves, to garnish

1 Heat the oil in a pan, then fry the onion for 5 minutes until soft. Stir in the spices. Add the courgette, tomato, chickpeas, raisins and stock, then bring to the boil. Cover and simmer for 10 minutes. Stir in the peas and cook for 5 minutes more. Sprinkle with coriander, to serve.

· ·
PER SERVING 294 kcals, protein 12g, carbs 35g, fat 9g, sat fat 1g, fibre 9g, sugar 19g, salt 0.6g

Sesame & honey tofu with rice noodles

High in protein and low in saturated fat, tofu is an excellent source of immune-boosting selenium. This Chinese-style stir fry is sure to become a firm favourite.

 45 minutes   2

- 1 tbsp rapeseed oil
- ½ x 396g pack firm tofu, cut into sticks and patted dry
- 75g/2½oz dried brown rice noodles
- 1 tsp toasted sesame oil
- 2 tsp reduced-salt light soy sauce
- 1 tsp Chinese five-spice powder
- 1 tsp clear honey
- 1 small red pepper, deseeded and thinly sliced
- ½ bunch spring onions, cut into fingers
- 1 head pak choi (about 100g/4oz), washed and leaves separated

1 Heat half the rapeseed oil in a frying pan over a medium heat. When hot, add the tofu and cook for 5 minutes on one side. Turn, then fry for another 3 minutes. Continue cooking for 10 minutes more, turning regularly – make sure you scrape up any bits that are stuck. Don't worry if the tofu falls apart a little – these pieces become crispy. Remove to a plate and keep warm.

2 Meanwhile, cook the noodles according to the pack instructions. Drain and set aside. Make the dressing by mixing the sesame oil, the soy sauce or tamari, five-spice and honey.

3 Heat the remaining oil in the frying pan and cook the pepper for 1 minute, then add the onions and pak choi. Toss together for 3 minutes, until just wilted. Add the noodles and half the dressing, and mix well. Heat through and divide between two bowls. Top with the tofu and drizzle over the remaining dressing.

PER SERVING 276 kcals, protein 13g, carbs 41g, fat 6g, sat fat 1g, fibre 3g, sugar 10g, salt 0.8g

Mediterranean fig & mozzarella salad

Smart enough to serve to fasting-day friends, this inventive salad certainly has the wow factor. Pour the wonderful dressing over the salad or serve it on the side.

 20 minutes 4

- 200g/8oz fine green beans, trimmed
- 6 small figs, quartered
- 1 shallot, thinly sliced
- 125g ball mozzarella, drained and ripped into chunks
- 50g/2oz hazelnuts, toasted and chopped
- small handful basil leaves, torn
- 3 tbsp balsamic vinegar
- 1 tbsp fig jam or relish
- 3 tbsp extra virgin olive oil

1 In a large pan of salted water, blanch the beans for 2–3 minutes. Drain, rinse in cold water, then drain on kitchen paper. Arrange the beans on a platter. Top with the figs, shallot, mozzarella, hazelnuts and basil.

2 In a small bowl or a jam jar with a fitted lid, put the vinegar, fig jam or relish, olive oil and some seasoning for the dressing. Mix or shake well and pour the dressing over the salad just before serving.

PER SERVING 286 kcals, protein 10g, carbs 11g, fat 23g, sat fat 6g, fibre 3g, sugar 9g, salt 0.3g

Feta & griddled-peach salad

Share this sweet and salty, fresh-tasting salad with fellow fasters. You can find jars of feta in oil at the cheese counter in most supermarkets. Keep some oil for the dressing.

 10 minutes   4

- oil, for greasing
- juice 1 lime
- 4 ripe peaches, each cut into wedges
- 200g bag mixed salad leaves
- 300g/10oz jar marinated feta in oil
- 1 red onion, sliced
- 2 tbsp chopped mint leaves

1 Heat a lightly greased griddle pan until very hot. Squeeze the lime juice over the peaches and put them on the griddle pan. Cook them for 2–3 minutes, turning, until nicely charred. Set aside.
2 In a large salad bowl, mix together the salad leaves, feta, 2 tablespoons of the oil from the feta, the sliced red onion and chopped mint. Season well.
3 Divide among plates and top with the charred peaches. Sprinkle over some freshly ground black pepper and serve warm.

PER SERVING 272 kcals, protein 11g, carbs 11g, fat 21g, sat fat 9g, fibre 2g, sugar 10g, salt 2.32g

Salmon noodle soup

Tinged with Eastern flavours, this soup is low in fat, heart healthy and a good source of omega-3 – plus it tastes sensational!

 35 minutes 2

- 500ml/18fl oz low-salt chicken stock
- 1 tsp Thai red curry paste
- 50g/2oz flat rice noodles
- 75g/2½oz shiitake mushrooms, sliced
- 50g/2oz baby corn, sliced
- 1 skinless salmon fillet, sliced
- juice 1 lime
- 1 tsp reduced-salt light soy sauce
- pinch brown sugar
- ½ small bunch coriander, leaves picked and chopped

1 Pour the stock into a large pan, bring to the boil, then stir in the curry paste. Add the noodles and cook for 8 minutes. Tip in the mushrooms and corn, and cook for 2 minutes more.

2 Add the salmon to the pan and cook for 3 minutes or until cooked through. Remove from the heat and stir in the lime juice, soy sauce and a pinch of sugar. Ladle into two bowls and sprinkle over the coriander just before serving.

PER SERVING 286 kcals, protein 26g, carbs 23g, fat 9g, sat fat 2g, fibre 2g, sugar 3g, salt 1.4g

Thai fried rice with prawns & peas

All the satisfaction of a big bowl of pad Thai but with better-for-you brown rice and veg.

 20 minutes 4

- 2 tbsp vegetable oil
- 1 red onion, halved and sliced
- 2 garlic cloves, sliced
- 1 red chilli, deseeded and sliced
- 250g/9oz large raw peeled prawns
- 300g/10oz cooked brown rice (about 140g/5oz uncooked)
- 75g/2½oz frozen peas
- 1 tbsp each reduced-salt light soy sauce and Thai fish sauce
- small bunch coriander, roughly chopped, plus a few leaves to garnish
- 4 eggs

1 Heat 1 tablespoon of the oil in a wok, add the onion, garlic and chilli, and cook for 2–3 minutes until golden. Add the prawns and cook for 1 minute.
2 Tip in the rice and peas, and keep tossing until very hot. Add the soy and fish sauces, then stir through the chopped coriander and keep warm.
3 Heat the remaining oil in a frying pan and fry the eggs with some seasoning. Divide the fried-rice mix among four bowls and top each with a fried egg. Serve scattered with coriander leaves.

PER SERVING 299 kcals, protein 24g, carbs 21g, fat 12g, sat fat 3g, fibre 3g, sugar 3g, salt 1.8g

Prawn & avocado salad with lime & chilli

Sweet, sour and spicy, this tangy salad will tantalise your taste buds.

 25 minutes   2

- 175g/6oz large cooked prawns, unpeeled but heads removed
- 1 avocado
- handful basil leaves, torn
- 60g bag baby leaf salad
- lime wedges, to garnish

FOR THE DRESSING
- 1 tbsp lime juice
- 1 tsp clear honey
- 1 red chilli, deseeded and finely chopped
- 1–2 tbsp light olive oil

1 Peel the prawns, leaving the tails intact, then rinse and pat dry. Set aside. Put all the dressing ingredients into a small bowl and whisk to mix.

2 Up to 1 hour before serving, peel and stone the avocado, then cut into thick slices and put in a large bowl with half the dressing. Mix lightly to coat all the slices (this prevents them turning brown).

3 Add the basil to the dressed avocado along with the prawns. Toss everything together.

4 Scatter the baby salad leaves on serving plates, then spoon over the prawns, avocado and basil mix. Drizzle with the remaining dressing and serve with lime wedges for squeezing over.

PER SERVING 274 kcals, protein 15g, carbs 5g, fat 21g, sat fat 4g, fibre 3g, sugar 4g, salt 1.4g

Crunchy prawn–noodle salad

The flavourful Vietnamese-style dressing for this crunchy salad is best made just before serving to preserve the vibrant colour of the mint.

 20 minutes   2

- 100g/4oz rice noodles
- 100g/4oz sugar-snap peas, shredded
- 2 carrots, coarsely grated
- 100g/4oz baby leaf spinach
- 85g/3oz cooked peeled prawns (defrosted if frozen)

FOR THE DRESSING

- 1 red chilli, deseeded and finely chopped
- 3 tbsp rice vinegar
- 1 tsp caster sugar
- 1 tsp Thai fish sauce
- 1 tbsp roughly chopped mint leaves

1 Pour boiling water over the noodles to cover, leave for 4 minutes, then cool under cold running water. Drain well.
2 Mix the sugar-snaps, carrots, spinach, noodles and prawns in a shallow bowl. Mix together the dressing ingredients until the sugar has dissolved, then pour the dressing over the salad and toss everything together. Serve straight away.

PER SERVING 278 kcals, protein 15g, carbs 55g, fat 1g, sat fat none, fibre 4g, sugar 13g, salt 1.43g

Sticky cod with celeriac & parsley mash

Ditch the Friday-night fish and chips – this lightly fried cod fillet is tasty and satisfying, while the celeriac is a low-carb alternative to potatoes.

 35 minutes 4

- 2 tbsp olive oil
- 4 x 120g/4½oz pieces cod fillet
- plain flour, for dusting
- 2 garlic cloves, chopped
- 1 tsp crushed chilli flakes
- 3 tbsp sherry vinegar
- 1 tbsp light soft brown sugar
- lemon wedges, to garnish

FOR THE MASH

- 1 large head celeriac (about 500g/1lb 2oz), peeled and cubed
- 2 tbsp butter
- big handful parsley leaves, finely chopped

1 To make the mash, boil the celeriac in salted water for 10 minutes until soft. Drain, put back in the pan and steam-dry for a few minutes. Mash with the butter and some seasoning, then stir in most of the parsley. Keep warm while you cook the fish.

2 Heat half the oil in a frying pan. Dust the fish in flour, season on both sides and fry for about 4 minutes on each side. Remove to a plate. Add the remaining oil to the pan and cook the garlic and chilli for 2 minutes until golden. Add the vinegar, sugar and a little salt, then allow to bubble for 1–2 minutes. Return the fish to the pan to warm through.

3 Serve the fish on the mash, with the sauce from the pan poured over. Sprinkle with the remaining parsley and serve with lemon wedges to squeeze over.

PER SERVING 259 kcals, protein 25g, carbs 10g, fat 13g, sat fat 5g, fibre 7g, sugar 7g, salt 0.6g

Fragrant fish tagine

Special enough for entertaining yet light enough to fit in with your fasting diet. Serve to non-fasters with basmati rice boiled with a little saffron. Any leftovers freeze well.

 1 hour 8

FOR THE CHERMOULA & FISH

- 2 tbsp olive oil
- 4 garlic cloves, chopped
- 4 tsp ground cumin
- 2 tsp paprika
- bunch coriander, chopped
- juice and zest 1 lemon
- 8 x 100g/4oz skinless tilapia fillets

FOR THE TAGINE

- 2 tbsp olive oil
- 2 large onions, thinly sliced
- 2 garlic cloves, sliced
- 2 tsp each ground cumin and paprika
- 3 x 400g cans chopped tomatoes
- 500ml/18fl oz fish stock
- 175g/6oz pimento-stuffed olives
- 4 green peppers, deseeded and sliced
- 500g bag baby new potatoes, halved lengthways

1 To make the chermoula, put the oil, garlic, cumin, paprika, three-quarters of the coriander and some seasoning in a small bowl. Add the lemon juice, then blitz with a hand blender until smooth. Spoon half of the chermoula over the fish fillets and turn them over to coat both sides. Set aside to marinate.

2 Heat the oil for the tagine in a large pan and fry the onions and garlic until softened and starting to colour, about 4–5 minutes. Add the cumin and paprika, and cook for 2 minutes more. Add the tomatoes, stock, olives and lemon zest, stir in the remaining chermoula and simmer, uncovered, for 10 minutes.

3 Stir in the peppers and potatoes, cover and simmer for 15 minutes until the potatoes are tender.

4 Stir the remaining coriander into the tagine, then arrange the fish fillets on top, and simmer gently for 4–6 minutes until the fish is just cooked and ready to serve.

PER SERVING 282 kcals, protein 24g, carbs 24g, fat 11g, sat fat 2g, fibre 5g, sugar 7g, salt 2.76g

Salmon with miso vegetables

Oil-rich fish like salmon is a real superfood – the healthy omega-3 fats are not only good for the heart but also make hair shine, eyes bright and skin healthy.

 15 minutes 2

- 18g packet miso soup mix
- 2 garlic cloves, finely grated
- 1 tbsp rice vinegar or white wine vinegar
- 100g/4oz thin-stemmed broccoli, cut into lengths and small florets
- 4 spring onions, chopped
- 100g/4oz beansprouts
- 2 big handfuls watercress (about 50–85g/2–3oz total)
- 240g pack skinless salmon fillets (2 per pack)

1 Make up the soup mix in a large pan with 500ml/18fl oz water and bring to the boil with the garlic and vinegar. Add the broccoli and spring onions, cover and cook for 5 minutes.
2 Stir in the beansprouts and watercress, top with the salmon and cover again. Cook for 4 minutes until the salmon flakes easily. Serve in bowls with a fork and spoon.

PER SERVING 282 kcals, protein 31g, carbs 6g, fat 15g, sat fat 3g, fibre 4g, sugar 4g, salt 1.2g

Spiced cod with quinoa salad & mint chutney

Filling yet low in fat and calories, white fish is a great choice for a fasting day.

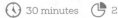 30 minutes   2

- 40g/1½oz quinoa (or 85g/3oz pre-cooked), rinsed
- 3 tbsp each chopped mint and coriander leaves
- 150g pot 0% natural yogurt
- 1 garlic clove
- ¼ tsp turmeric powder
- pinch cumin seeds
- 2 x 150g chunky skinless white fish fillets, such as sustainable cod
- ¼ cucumber, finely diced
- 1 small red onion, finely chopped
- 4 tomatoes, chopped
- good squeeze lemon juice

1 Tip the quinoa (if not pre-cooked) into a pan, cover with water then boil, covered, for 25 minutes, checking the water level to make sure it doesn't boil dry. Drain well.

2 Meanwhile, put 2 tablespoons each of the mint and coriander in a bowl. Add the yogurt and garlic, and blitz with a hand blender until smooth. Stir 2 tablespoons of the mint chutney with the turmeric and cumin, then add the fish and turn in the mixture completely to coat it.

3 Turn grill to high. Arrange the fish in a shallow heatproof dish and grill for 8–10 minutes, depending on the thickness, until it flakes. Toss the quinoa with the cucumber, onion, tomatoes, lemon juice and remaining herbs. Spoon the quinoa salad on to a plate, add the fish and spoon round the mint chutney or serve it alongside.

PER SERVING 272 kcals, protein 36g, carbs 24g, fat 3g, sat fat 1g, fibre 2g, sugar 12g, salt 0.4g

Fish-pie fillets

. . . .

These filo-topped fish fillets are supereasy to make and perfect for a great family supper. Just serve with new potatoes for non-fasters.

 20 minutes, plus defrosting 4

- 4 x 175g/6oz thick white fish fillets (such as haddock)
- small bunch dill, leaves only, chopped
- 100g/4oz half-fat soft cheese
- 200g/8oz frozen prawns, raw or cooked, defrosted
- 4 sheets filo pastry
- 2 tsp sunflower oil
- 1 tbsp finely grated Parmesan
- green salad, to serve (optional)

1 Heat oven to 220C/200C fan/gas 7. Put the fish on to a non-stick baking sheet and season all over. Mix the dill and soft cheese in a small bowl, then stir in the prawns, taking care not to break them up. Season with black pepper, then spread evenly over the fish.

2 Brush the filo sheets with the oil, then cut into thick strips. Scrunch up the pastry a little and crumple it on top of the fish. Scatter with Parmesan, then bake for 10 minutes or until the fish is cooked through and the pastry is crisp and golden. (If you've used raw prawns, check they're cooked through properly.) Serve with a simple green salad, if you like.

. . . .

PER FILLET 296 kcals, protein 46g, carbs 13g, fat 7g, sat fat 3g, fibre none, sugar 2g, salt 1.3g

Sesame-chicken salad

This warm chicken salad, tossed through a fragrant sweet–sour Asian sauce packs a powerful protein-punch.

 20 minutes   2

- 2 boneless skinless chicken breasts
- 85g/3oz frozen soya beans
- 1 large carrot, finely cut into thin matchsticks
- 4 spring onions, finely sliced
- 140g/5oz cherry tomatoes, halved
- small bunch coriander, chopped small
- handful Thai or ordinary basil leaves, torn if large
- 85g/3oz herb or baby salad leaves
- 1 tsp toasted sesame seeds

FOR THE DRESSING
- grated zest and juice 1 small lime
- 1 tsp Thai fish sauce
- 1 tsp sesame oil
- 2 tsp sweet chilli sauce

1 Put the chicken in a pan then pour over cold water to cover. Tip the soya beans into a steamer. Bring the pan to a gentle simmer then cook the chicken for 8 minutes with the beans in the steamer above.

2 Meanwhile, mix the dressing ingredients in a large bowl. When the chicken is cooked, slice and toss in the dressing with the beans, carrot, onions, tomatoes, coriander and basil. Mix really well, then pile on to the salad leaves and sprinkle with the sesame seeds to serve.

PER SERVING 300 kcals, protein 44g, carbs 14g, fat 7g, sat fat 1g, fibre 6g, sugar 12g, salt 1g

Squash & chorizo stew

· ·

· A quick low-fat casserole that's as easy to make for a crowd or the freezer as it is just for one.

 35 minutes 4

- 140g/5oz chorizo sausage, thickly sliced
- 1 onion, chopped
- 680g jar passata
- 1 butternut squash (about 1kg/2lb 4oz), peeled and cut into 1–2cm/½–¾in chunks
- handful flat-leaf parsley, chopped

1 Heat a large pan, add the chorizo, then cook over a high heat for 2 minutes or until it starts to release its red oil. Lift the chorizo out of the pan on to a plate, then add the onion to the pan and fry for 5 minutes until starting to soften.

2 Tip the passata, squash and chorizo into the pan, bring to the boil, then cover and cook for 15–20 minutes or until the squash is softened, but not broken up. If you need to, add a little water during cooking. Season to taste, then serve in bowls scattered with the chopped parsley.

· ·
PER SERVING 264 kcals, protein 13g, carbs 35g, fat 9g, sat fat 4g, fibre 5g, sugar 19g, salt 2.17g

Asian beef & watercress salad

The pepperiness of watercress works well with Asian flavours. If you like cucumber, add it instead of some of the mango to give this tasty salad low-calorie crunchiness.

 30 minutes 🥧 2

- 250g/9oz lean stir-fry beef, cubed
- 1–2 tsp Thai fish sauce
- juice 1 lime
- small piece ginger, peeled and finely chopped
- 1 garlic clove, crushed
- 1 small red chilli, deseeded and finely chopped
- 1 tbsp soft brown sugar
- bunch watercress
- ½ mango, peeled and cut into medium chunks
- ½ small red onion, thinly sliced into ½ moons
- 1 tsp vegetable oil

1 Season the beef with some black pepper and a little of the fish sauce and set aside.
2 In a small bowl, mix together the lime juice, ginger, garlic, chilli, brown sugar and remaining fish sauce. Taste for extra seasoning – it should be sweet, salty and sour without any one flavour being dominant.
3 Put a handful of watercress on each serving plate, then divide the mango chunks and red onion among the leaves.
4 Just before serving, set a wok over a high heat and drizzle in the oil. Sear the meat, turning often until browned all over. Divide among the plates of salad and pour over the dressing. Serve while warm.

PER SERVING 287 kcals, protein 26g, carbs 23g, fat 9g, sat fat 3g, fibre 3g, sugar 22g, salt 0.98g

Goulash in a dash

Minute steak is great for weeknight family suppers as it's so quick to cook. It's also very lean, so lower in fat than other cuts. For non-fasters, serve with rice or crusty bread.

 30 minutes 4

- 1 tbsp vegetable oil
- 300g/10oz stir-fry beef strips or minute steak cut into strips
- 100g/4oz chestnut mushrooms, quartered
- 2 tsp paprika
- 500g/1lb 2oz potatoes, peeled and cut into smallish chunks
- 600ml/1 pint hot beef stock (a cube is fine)
- 500g jar tomato-based cooking sauce
- handful parsley leaves, roughly chopped
- few swirls natural yogurt, to garnish

1 Heat half the oil in a large non-stick pan and fry the beef for 2 minutes, stirring once halfway through. Tip the meat on to a plate. Heat the remaining oil in the pan (there is no need to clean it) and fry the mushrooms for 2–3 minutes until they start to colour.

2 Sprinkle the paprika over the mushrooms, fry briefly, then tip in the potatoes, stock and tomato sauce. Give it all a good stir, then cover and simmer for 20 minutes until the potatoes are tender. Return the beef to the pan along with any juices and warm through. Stir in the parsley and a swirl of yogurt, and serve.

PER SERVING 299 kcals, protein 23g, carbs 33g, fat 9g, sat fat 2g, fibre 3g, sugar 5g, salt 1.59g

Beef stir fry with broccoli & oyster sauce

Beef stir-fry strips are handy, but you can also slice your own steaks. Put steaks in the freezer for 10 minutes then cut into slices.

 15 minutes 2

- 1–2 tbsp sunflower oil
- 200g/8oz beef stir-fry strips
- 200g pack Tenderstem broccoli
- 1 onion, sliced
- 2 garlic cloves, sliced
- 2 tbsp oyster sauce

1 Heat a wok until smoking, pour in the oil then add the beef. Stir-fry for 2 minutes, then tip the beef on to a plate. Add the broccoli to the wok with a splash of water then cook until it turns bright green.

2 Add the onion to the wok and stir-fry for 1 minute, then add the garlic and cook for 1 minute more. Pour in the oyster sauce and 125ml/4fl oz water. Bring to the boil and cook until reduced to a sticky sauce. Stir in the beef, along with any juices from the plate, then serve straight away.

PER SERVING 256 kcals, protein 30g, carbs 10g, fat 12g, sat fat 2g, fibre 4g, sugar 8g, salt 1.78g

Summer soufflé omelette

By separating the eggs and whisking the whites, this recipe gives you an altogether lighter omelette.

 15 minutes 2

- 4 eggs
- 1 tbsp grated Parmesan
- small handful basil leaves, finely shredded
- 1 tbsp olive oil
- 50g/2oz goat's cheese, broken into chunks
- 4 cherry tomatoes, halved

1 Heat grill to high. Crack the eggs, then separate the yolks from the whites into two bowls. Tip the Parmesan and most of the basil in with the yolks and season. Whisk the whites vigorously for about a minute or until light and fluffy, then, using the same whisk, beat the yolks with the Parmesan and basil. Finally, whisk the yolk mix into the egg whites.

2 Heat the oil in a small frying pan and tip in the egg mix. Leave to cook for a minute, then scatter over the goat's cheese and tomatoes.

3 Put the pan under the grill for 5 minutes or until puffed up, golden and set with only the slightest wobble. Scatter over the remaining basil leaves and serve.

PER SERVING 302 kcals, protein 20g, carbs 1g, fat 24g, sat fat 8g, fibre none, sugar 2g, salt 0.81g

Spiced tortilla

· ·

Indian spices and eggs work together brilliantly in this filling veggie meal. Chill leftovers and enjoy them for lunch the next day.

 25 minutes   4

- 1 tbsp sunflower oil
- 1 onion, sliced
- 1 red chilli, deseeded and shredded
- 2 tsp ground curry spices (we mixed coriander, cumin and turmeric)
- 300g/10oz cherry tomatoes
- 500g/1lb 2oz cooked potatoes, sliced
- bunch coriander, stalks finely chopped, leaves roughly chopped
- 8 eggs, beaten

1 Heat the oil in a large frying pan. Fry the onion and half the chilli for 5 minutes until softened. Tip in the curry spices, fry for 1 minute more, then add the cherry tomatoes, potatoes and coriander stalks to the pan. Season the eggs well, pour over the top of the veg and leave to cook gently for 8–10 minutes until almost set.

2 Heat the grill to high and flash the tortilla underneath it for 1–2 minutes until the top is set. Scatter the coriander leaves and remaining chilli over the top, slice into wedges and serve.

· ·
PER SERVING 327 kcals, protein 19g, carbs 27g, fat 17g, sat fat 4g, fibre 3g, sugar 5g, salt 0.69g

Puy-lentil salad with soya beans, sugar-snaps & broccoli

The delicious sesame dressing for this tasty salad adds zing to the vibrant veg. Keep leftovers for a delicious instant lunch the next day.

 25 minutes 4

- 200g/8oz Puy lentils
- 1 litre/1¾ pints hot vegetable stock
- 200g/8oz Tenderstem broccoli
- 140g/5oz frozen soya beans, thawed
- 140g/5oz sugar-snap peas
- 1 red chilli, deseeded and sliced

FOR THE DRESSING
- 2 tbsp sesame oil
- juice 1 lemon
- 1 garlic clove, chopped
- 2½ tbsp reduced-salt light soy sauce
- 3cm/1¼in piece ginger, finely grated
- 1 tbsp clear honey

1 Boil the lentils in the stock for about 15 minutes until just cooked. Drain, then tip into a large bowl. Bring a pan of salted water to the boil, throw in the broccoli for 1 minute, add the beans and peas for 1 minute more. Drain, then cool under cold water. Pat dry, then add to the bowl with the lentils.

2 Mix together the dressing ingredients with some seasoning. Pour the dressing over the lentils and vegetables, then mix in well with the sliced chilli and serve.

PER SERVING 302 kcals, protein 22g, carbs 42g, fat 7g, sat fat 1g, fibre 8g, sugar 9g, salt 1.41g

Soba noodle & edamame salad with grilled tofu

Edamame (or soya) beans can be bought fresh or frozen and are packed with goodness. They have a slightly nutty taste – swap them for broad beans, if you prefer.

 30 minutes   2

- 50g/2oz soba noodles
- 140g/5oz fresh or frozen podded edamame (soya) beans
- 2 spring onions, shredded
- 140g/5oz beansprouts
- ½ cucumber, peeled, deseeded and sliced
- 1 tsp sesame oil
- 125g block firm tofu, patted dry and thickly sliced
- 1 tsp vegetable oil
- handful coriander leaves, to garnish

FOR THE DRESSING

- 1–2 tbsp mirin (rice wine)
- 1 tsp reduced-salt light soy sauce
- 1 tbsp orange juice
- 1 red chilli, deseeded (optional) and finely chopped

1 Heat the dressing ingredients together in your smallest pan, simmer for just 30 seconds, then set aside and keep warm.
2 Boil the noodles according to the pack instructions, adding the edamame beans for the final 2 minutes of the cooking time. Rinse under very cold water, drain thoroughly and tip into a large bowl with the spring onions, beansprouts, cucumber, sesame oil and warm dressing. Season, if you like.
3 Heat grill to high. Brush the tofu with the vegetable oil, season and grill (or griddle) for 2–3 minutes each side – the tofu is very delicate so turn it carefully. Top the salad with the tofu, scatter with coriander leaves and serve.

PER SERVING 328 kcals, protein 21g, carbs 30g, fat 12g, sat fat 2g, fibre 7g, sugar 8g, salt 0.8g

Warm squash salad with garlic vinaigrette

Sweet and satisfying, roasted butternut squash works incredibly well with the vinaigrette in this sensational salad.

 35 minutes 2

- ½ small butternut squash, peeled, deseeded and sliced into 3cm/1¼in pieces
- 2 tbsp olive oil, plus extra to grease
- 1 big handful rocket leaves
- 125g ball mozzarella, torn

FOR THE VINAIGRETTE

- 1 garlic clove, thinly sliced
- 1 tbsp red wine vinegar
- 1 tsp honey
- small handful mint leaves, chopped

1 Heat oven to 200C/180C fan/gas 6. Put the squash pieces on a large, greased baking sheet and drizzle with 1 tablespoon of the oil. Season well and roast for 25 minutes or until golden.

2 While the squash is roasting, make the vinaigrette. Heat the remaining oil in a small pan. Add the garlic, keeping the heat low, and cook until golden. Remove from the heat and add the vinegar and honey. Return to the heat for 1 minute, whisking until the vinaigrette becomes syrupy.

3 To serve, arrange the rocket and mozzarella on individual plates. Add the mint to the vinaigrette. Divide the squash between the plates and drizzle with the warm vinaigrette.

PER SERVING 334 kcals, protein 13g, carbs 15g, fat 24g, sat fat 10g, fibre 3g, sugar 9g, salt 0.65g

Quinoa stew with squash & pomegranate

This one-pot needs no accompaniments, so you can enjoy a filling supper for less than 320 calories per person!

 55 minutes   4

- 1 small butternut squash, peeled, deseeded and cubed
- 2 tbsp olive oil
- 1 large onion, thinly sliced
- 1 garlic clove, chopped
- 1 tbsp ginger, peeled and finely chopped
- 1 tsp ras-el-hanout or Moroccan spice mix
- 200g/8oz quinoa, rinsed
- 5 prunes, roughly chopped
- juice 1 lemon
- 600ml/1 pint vegetable stock
- seeds from 1 pomegranate and small handful mint leaves, to garnish

1 Heat oven to 200C/180C fan/gas 6. Put the squash on a baking sheet and toss with 1 tablespoon of the oil. Season well and roast for 30–35 minutes, or until soft.

2 Meanwhile, heat the remaining oil in a big pan. Add the onion, garlic and ginger, season and cook for 10 minutes. Add the spice mix and quinoa, and cook for another couple of minutes. Add the prunes, lemon juice and stock, bring to the boil, then cover and simmer for 25 minutes.

3 When everything is tender, stir the squash through the stew. Spoon into bowls and scatter with pomegranate seeds and mint to serve. Keep any leftovers for a satisfying lunch next day.

PER SERVING 318 kcals, protein 11g, carbs 50g, fat 9g, sat fat 1g, fibre 6g, sugar 20g, salt 0.5g

Rigatoni with rich mushroom sauce

Chestnut mushrooms add masses of flavour to this family-friendly, low-fat pasta dish, which will also provide you with one of your 5-a-day.

🕐 25 minutes 4

- ½ x 40g pack dried mushrooms
- 300g/10oz rigatoni
- 2 tsp olive oil
- 1 red onion, finely chopped
- 300g/10oz chestnut mushrooms, sliced
- few thyme sprigs or good pinch dried thyme
- 2 tsp tomato purée

1 Soak the dried mushrooms in 175ml/6fl oz boiling water. Cook the pasta in a large pan of boiling water, according to the pack instructions.

2 Meanwhile, heat the oil in a pan, add the onion and fry gently for 5 minutes until softened. Drain the soaked mushrooms, reserving the soaking liquid, and finely chop. Stir the fresh and soaked mushrooms, thyme and tomato purée into the onion, then add 150ml/¼ pint of the mushroom-soaking liquid, discarding the remainder. Bring to the boil.

3 Reduce the heat and simmer for 5 minutes until the mushrooms are tender. Drain the pasta, return to the pan and combine with the mushroom sauce to serve.

PER SERVING 304 kcals, protein 12g, carbs 60g, fat 4g, sat fat 1g, fibre 4g, sugar 4g, salt 0.06g

Smoked trout, beetroot & horseradish flatbreads

· ·

Crisp wraps work really well as light pizza-style bases and make a popular lunch for all the family. Try this Scandi topping, then experiment with your own favourites.

 18 minutes   4

- 4 flatbreads
- olive oil, for brushing
- 2 tbsp horseradish sauce
- 2 tbsp crème fraîche
- small bunch dill, ½ chopped, ½ picked into small fronds
- squeeze lemon juice, plus pinch zest
- 3 cooked beetroots (not in vinegar), very thinly sliced
- 4 smoked trout fillets, broken into large flakes
- salad leaves, to serve (optional)

1 Heat oven to 220C/200C fan/gas 7. Brush the flatbreads with olive oil. Put the oiled breads on a large baking sheet and pop in the oven for about 8 minutes until crisp round the edges.

2 Meanwhile, mix the horseradish, crème fraîche, chopped dill, lemon juice and zest and some seasoning in a small jug or bowl to make a sauce. Add a few drops of water to loosen the mixture to a drizzling consistency.

3 Top each flatbread with some beetroot slices and one of the smoked trout fillets. Drizzle over the horseradish sauce, sprinkle with dill fronds and serve with salad, if you like.

· ·

PER FLATBREAD 327 kcals, protein 21g, carbs 42g, fat 10g, sat fat 4g, fibre 3g, sugar 5g, salt 2.1g

Oaty fish & prawn gratins

A classic fish pie with a creamy mash-topping is packed with calories, but these crumb-topped versions are much healthier.

 40 minutes   2

- 340g bag baby leaf spinach, roughly chopped
- 400g can chopped tomatoes with garlic and herbs
- 200g/8oz sustainable white fish fillets, chopped into large chunks
- small bunch basil leaves, shredded
- 100g/4oz cooked peeled prawns
- 1 tbsp finely grated Parmesan
- 1 tbsp breadcrumbs
- 1 tbsp rolled oats
- broccoli, boiled or steamed, to serve

1 Put the spinach in a large colander and pour over some boiling water. Once cool enough to handle, squeeze out any excess water, then season and set aside.

2 Heat oven to 220C/200C fan/gas 7. Tip the tomatoes into a frying pan with some seasoning and simmer for 5 minutes to thicken. Add the fish and heat for 1–2 minutes – it doesn't need to be fully cooked at this point. Stir in the basil.

3 Divide the prawns, spinach, fish and tomato sauce between two gratin dishes. Mix the Parmesan, breadcrumbs and oats together, and sprinkle evenly over the top of both gratin dishes. Bake for 20 minutes until golden and bubbling. Serve with the cooked broccoli.

PER GRATIN 343 kcals, protein 43g, carbs 25g, fat 6g, sat fat 2g, fibre 8g, sugar 9g, salt 2.1g

Chicken tikka with spiced rice

Much healthier than your average takeaway, this delicious version of an all-time favourite makes a great choice for fasting Fridays.

🕐 30 minutes, plus marinating and chilling   4

- 4 boneless skinless chicken breasts
- 150g pot low-fat natural yogurt
- 50g/2oz tikka masala curry paste
- 100g/4oz cucumber, diced
- 1 tbsp roughly chopped mint leaves
- 1 red onion, cut into thin wedges
- 140g/5oz easy cook long grain rice
- 1 tbsp medium curry powder
- 50g/2oz frozen peas
- 1 small red pepper, deseeded and diced

1 Slash each chicken breast deeply with a knife three to four times on one side. Put in a bowl and add 50g/2oz of the yogurt and the tikka paste. Mix well, cover and marinate in the fridge for 30 minutes. Make the raita by stirring the cucumber and most of the mint into the rest of the yogurt. Season, cover and chill.

2 Heat oven to 240C/220C fan/gas 9. Scatter the onion over a foil-lined baking sheet. Remove the chicken from the marinade, shake off any excess and put the chicken on top of the onion. Put in the oven for 20 minutes.

3 Meanwhile, tip the rice, curry powder, peas and pepper into a pan of boiling water, and simmer for 10 minutes or until the rice is just tender. Drain well and divide the rice among four plates. Add the roasted chicken and onion and sprinkle over the remaining mint. Serve with the cucumber raita alongside.

PER SERVING 342 kcals, protein 37g, carbs 38g, fat 5g, sat fat 1g, fibre 4g, sugar 7g, salt 0.7g

Chicken breast with avocado salad

The heat of the smoked paprika contrasts well with the coolness of the salad in this superspeedy meal. The salad can be easily doubled.

 20 minutes  1

- 1 boneless skinless chicken breast
- 2 tsp olive oil
- 1 heaped tsp smoked paprika

FOR THE SALAD
- ½ small avocado, diced
- 1 medium tomato, chopped
- ½ small red onion, thinly sliced
- 1 tsp red wine vinegar
- 1 tbsp roughly chopped flat-leaf parsley

1 Heat grill to medium. Rub the chicken all over with 1 teaspoon of the olive oil and the paprika. Grill the chicken for 4–5 minutes on each side until lightly charred and cooked through.

2 Mix together the avocado, tomato and red onion for the salad. Whisk together the remaining oil, the vinegar, parsley and some seasoning, and drizzle over the salad. Thickly slice the chicken and serve with the avocado salad.

PER SERVING 344 kcals, protein 32g, carbs 9g, fat 20g, sat fat 4g, fibre 3g, sugar 5g, salt 0.23g

Minced beef & sweet potato stew

Thrifty lean mince makes a great base for a hearty, but healthy, family casserole.
Serve simply with your favourite seasonal greens.

 20 minutes 4

- 1 tbsp sunflower oil
- 1 large onion, chopped
- 1 large carrot, chopped
- 1 celery stick, sliced
- 500g/1lb 2oz lean beef mince
- 1 tbsp each tomato purée and mushroom ketchup
- 400g can chopped tomatoes
- 450g/1lb sweet potatoes, peeled and cut into large chunks
- few thyme sprigs
- 1 bay leaf
- handful parsley, leaves chopped

1 Heat the oil in a large pan, sweat the onion, carrot and celery for 10 minutes until soft. Then add the beef and cook until it is browned all over.
2 Add the tomato purée and cook for a few minutes, then add the mushroom ketchup, tomatoes, sweet potatoes, herbs and a can of water. Season well and bring to the boil.
3 Simmer for 40–45 minutes on a low heat until the sweet potatoes are tender, stirring a few times throughout to make sure they are cooking evenly.
4 Once cooked, remove the bay leaf, stir through the chopped parsley and serve with seasonal greens.

PER SERVING 368 kcals, protein 29g, carbs 35g, fat 13g, sat fat 5g, fibre 6g, sugar 17g, salt 0.6g

Index

Also available from BBC Books and Good Food

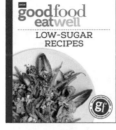

Try 3 issues for just £3

Subscribe to **BBC Good Food magazine** for inspired ideas, reliable recipes and practical tips for all home cooks. Whether you're passionate about cooking, or just love eating good food and trying out a few easy recipes, **BBC Good Food** is the magazine for you.

Every issue includes:

★ **Triple tested recipes**

★ **Inspiring ideas**

★ **Mouth-watering photography**

★ **PLUS** as subscriber you'll receive **exclusive covers** and subscriber only offers

Subscribe today and trial your first 3 issues of BBC Good Food magazine for just £3*